Philippians & Philemon
Bill Ireland

Colossians
Dock Hollingsworth

Also by Bill Ireland

Daniel Annual Bible Study

Dedication

*To my wife, Ginny,
my full partner
in the gospel of Jesus Christ*

Bill

*For Melissa,
God's life-giving gift*

Dock

Contents

Part 1: Philippians

Acknowledgements	3
Preface	5
1. Location, Location, Location	7
2. No Unfinished Business	13
3. Praying Life: Doing What's Best	19
4. Interpreting My Chains	25
5. Thinking Out Loud	31
6. Worthy of the Gospel	37
7. Get Your Mind Right!	43
8. Climbing Down the Ladder	49
9. Working It Out	55
10. Between Hope and Necessity	61
11. Thwarting Sabotage	67
12. A Threat to Faith: Excessive Spirituality	73
13. Living Up to Our Name	79
14. Antidote for Anxiety	85
15. Thinking and Doing	91
16. Learning the Secret	97
17. Provision for Our Needs	103
18. Last Words	109

Part 2: Philemon

1. The Church in Your House	117
2. What Good Can I Do?	123
3. Doing the Hard Thing	127

Part 3: Colossians

1. Getting Word to the Saints and the Faithful	135
2. Getting Out of the Darkness	141
3. Getting Clear about Christ	147
4. Getting the Mystery Revealed	153
5. Getting from Captivity to the Cross	159
6. Getting Free from the World to Make a Difference	165
7. Getting Dressed for Abundant Living	171
8. Getting Relationships in Order	177
9. Getting a Little Help from My Friends	183

Part 1

Philippians

by Bill Ireland

Acknowledgements

Although writing is a solitary process, writers invariably depend on others to help them see their projects through to completion. This project would not have begun to take shape without the kind and generous invitation from Keith Gammons to contribute to a new series. For his confidence, suggestions, and advice, I am most grateful. Katie Brookins of Smyth & Helwys made herself available whenever I had questions or needed suggestions. Her faithful attention insured that this project would see the light of day. I am also greatly indebted to Gail Stephenson, who retyped many of these original manuscripts after the electronic files had been lost. Her investment of time and energy was truly a gift of grace that prevented an overload of frustration and a subsequent loss of some of my religion! Her efforts enabled me to finish this work in a timely fashion. As always, the congregation of First Baptist Church of Dalton, Georgia, blessed my efforts to prepare these sermons for wider publication. They understood that my efforts to write demanded I shed some of my normal responsibilities for a time and retreat from the office, particularly as the deadline loomed closer. And finally, my most profound thanks are reserved for my wife, Ginny. She has been and continues to be my best critic, encourager, and listener. We are indeed, in Paul's words, "partners in the gospel," and she makes me better than I would have been on my own. Through her I catch frequent glimpses of the Christ whom we both try to serve. As a result of our partnership, I have more blessings than my hands or my heart can hold.

—Bill Ireland

Preface

Communication demands a lot of time and energy these days. Dispensing pertinent information in a timely manner is an ongoing challenge for any church. Even then, it can be a cause for table-banging frustration! For example, churches may produce a monthly news magazine, distribute a weekly e-news update, post events on social media, send out text blasts, print announcements in the weekly order of service, and make announcements from the pulpit. Posters and announcements displayed on electronic message boards offer constant reminders of upcoming events. Despite those efforts, the message doesn't always hit the target. Invariably, someone will say, "I didn't know a thing about that!" This development usually leads church staff members to throw up their hands and lament, "How could they miss it?" My hunch is that the information is missed simply because there's just too much information floating around out there to be absorbed. We just can't take it all in or make a connection with all of it.

Nevertheless, the precarious nature of passing along routine information often makes me wonder about the effectiveness of preaching. If people miss the date and time of a meeting, then how many times do they miss the message on Sunday? How does anyone ever "get" what is said from the pulpit? How does it ever hit home and make a difference? What does it take for the gospel to hit home?

The best answer I can come up with is this: the key difference between routine communication and meaningful preaching is that preaching involves a relationship between the pastor and the people. Routine information about meetings or retreats doesn't carry that kind of weight. The beauty of "preaching the gospel in context" is that over time the pastor and the people get to know one another. Relationships are formed. Life events are shared. As a result, the pastor learns how best to speak to his or her congregation. And, over time, the congregation learns how to listen to its minister. Preachers teach their congregations how to listen; congregations also teach preachers how best to speak to them. This dynamic gives preaching its true power and enables effective proclamation of the gospel. This dynamic allows the gospel to get a hearing in a world cluttered with messages and overloaded with information.

Certainly, among the best examples of this phenomenon in the New Testament are Paul's letters to the church at Philippi and to Philemon. These are among Paul's most intimate and personal letters. They give evidence of some heartfelt give and take between the apostle and those to whom he was writing. The relationships between Paul and his addressees are always in the foreground. Those relationships amplify the letters' content. My hope is that the sermons drawn from these two letters will underscore and highlight the personal element that makes them prime examples of "preaching the gospel in context."

The sermons in this volume were offered to two very fine congregations: Ardmore Baptist Church in Winston-Salem, North Carolina, and First Baptist Church in Dalton, Georgia. In both places, I was blessed with attentive listeners. I know their faithful attention made me better; my hope is that what they heard from me made them better as followers of Jesus Christ.

1

Location, Location, Location

Philippians 1:1-2

Introduction

Letter writing is rapidly becoming a lost art. Electronic correspondence has virtually (no pun intended!) replaced pen and paper messages. A trip to the mailbox rarely yields anything more than magazines, bills, credit-card offers, and sale circulars. A letter or card is a rare find!

I was reminded of this when my sister showed me a collection of letters my mother had saved throughout her life. There, on worn and fragile paper with fading ink, was a priceless record of her days upon this earth. Some of the letters traced the budding romance between her and our dad. Other letters were from friends and relatives that detailed mundane affairs such as shopping excursions, local gossip, and, of course, the weather. A few of the letters were ones she had written home while she was off at college, reporting to *her* parents how her classes were going and fervently promising to write more often. This worn collection reminded me that, throughout the ages, letters were written by and to real flesh-and-blood people.

Commentaries routinely feature a section on where a biblical letter's recipients were located. Honestly, this material tends to be rather dry except for those committed to rigorous scholarship. Nevertheless, the information does anchor a letter, opening a window into a particular place, its history, and the circumstances of its residents. Again, we give these matters attention because they remind us that the New Testament letter was written to real people trying to figure out how to live out their faith where they lived.

The letter to the church at Philippi was written to people not all that different from us. That's why I chose to give some attention to

Philippians 1:1-2 at the outset of this series of sermons. We tend to overlook a letter's greeting and address in our haste to get to its substance. Giving attention to "location, location, location," however, signals that while there is indeed historical distance between us and the original recipients, we actually have more in common than we imagine. Like those Philippian Christians of old, we have to figure out how to live out our faith in our zip code. Like those Philippian Christians, we too have to keep our eyes open for how God uses *where* we are to shape *who* we are.

Location, Location, Location

Most of us, I assume, have heard the cardinal rule of real estate, the one that trumps all others when it comes to buying property: location, location, location! Boiled down to its essentials, this dictum asserts that *where* a property is situated determines its value. A piece of land on the growing edge of a community will fetch a much higher price in ten years than a similar parcel on the other side of town. A house in the middle of nowhere usually isn't worth as much as one that affords the owner easy access to good schools and other services. Location is vital to the success of a proposed shopping center. If it's developed on or near a heavily traveled road, it stands a good chance of attracting customers. If it's too far off the beaten path and too difficult to get to, people will likely choose somewhere more convenient. The stores will struggle to turn a profit. "Where" is absolutely vital. Location is everything.

In that light, I have to remind you that every letter in the New Testament is addressed to a specific location, and the mailing address often helps us better understand the content of the letter itself. One of the most common mistakes we make in reading Scripture is to sever a particular document from its context. We forget we're literally reading other people's mail! Each letter was written to people who were located in a particular time and a particular place. As in our own day, no two churches were identical and neither were their struggles. The problems the Corinthians faced were very different from those faced by the folks in Colossae or Galatia. The letter to the Ephesians has an entirely different feel and tone than the letter to Philemon. Without exception, all the letters had a specific destination and were written to people who were trying to figure out *how* to be a follower of Jesus Christ in their particular setting. They were seeking to match their faith with their location.

Such is true in Paul's letter to the Philippians, undoubtedly the warmest and most intimate of his epistles. Look closely for a moment at how the apostle begins this letter. It is addressed to *all the saints in Christ Jesus who are in Philippi* (v. 1). Literally, Paul wrote "to all the saints, the ones who are in Philippi." In Philippi! That was the location of the church, and one thing is for sure: it was a difficult place to be a believer.

According to the book of Acts, the church in Philippi encountered trouble right from the start (16:11-40). When Paul and Silas arrived in Philippi, they began looking for opportunities to preach the gospel. One Sabbath they found a group of women who had gathered beside the river for prayer. One of the women was Lydia, a dealer in purple cloth. As a result of Paul's preaching, she received the gospel and was baptized. So profound was the impact of the good news upon her life that she opened her home as a base for the apostles' ministry.

It was a great start, but it didn't last long. Shortly thereafter, things went downhill. As Paul and Silas continued their ministry in Philippi, a young slave girl who was possessed by an evil spirit followed them everywhere. She pestered Paul to no end, and eventually Paul became so exasperated and angry that he cast the spirit out of her. Good news, right? Not exactly! This slave girl was a moneymaker for her owners. Her ability to tell fortunes ensured they had a steady supply of willing customers, customers who would pay a price to uncover their future. When Paul cast the evil spirit out of her, she lost her power and her owners' source of income quickly dried up. As a result, they seized Paul and Silas and arrested them, charging them with disturbing the peace and slandering them as outsiders and traitors to Rome. The authorities accepted all those charges at face value and, without even the semblance of a trial, had Paul and Silas flogged and thrown into jail.

That night, however, a great earthquake shook the prison, and Paul used the opportunity to preach the gospel to their jailer, who believed and was baptized along with his entire household. The next day, the authorities intended to let them go quietly, but Paul called attention to the injustice they had suffered, invoking their rights as Roman citizens. The authorities apologized but still asked them to leave the city. Paul and Silas came to the conclusion that they had worn out their welcome and that staying would be detrimental to the church. So, they departed, leaving the fledging congregation to fend for itself, but also promising to keep in touch. The apostles' departure, however, wasn't the end of the church's troubles. Left without leadership, this young church struggled to bear witness in a hostile environment, a fact Paul will allude to several times in this letter.

As bad as all that was, the environment on the *outside* of the church wasn't all that made things difficult. The environment on the *inside* was just as problematic. Notice again Paul's phrasing: *To* all *the saints*.... That word "all" pops up repeatedly in this letter, and its appearance is anything but accidental. As we work our way through this letter, we will see that this beloved congregation was not only beset by trouble from without but also from within. Something—we're not exactly sure what—was tearing at the fabric of their life together. There was dissension and friction, and their unity was fraying at the edges.

Paul's clearest allusion to their strife shows up in the opening verses of the fourth chapter where he names names! He calls on Euodia and Syntyche "to be of the same mind" (Philippians 4:2). In other words, the apostle urged these two to stop their bickering and put aside their differences. No wonder, then, that Paul, in his efforts to help this church stay together, stressed "all"—all the saints, all of you, all the brothers and sisters. No one left out. No one excluded. For better or for worse, all the members of this church were stuck with each other. And, whatever their challenges, they would have to work them out *together*.

No, Philippi wasn't an easy place, and sometimes the members of the church itself added to their difficulty. In spite of all that, they would have to keep living out their faith right there *in* Philippi. In Philippi and not someplace else! By means of this simple address, Paul wouldn't let them forget that they had been called to be God's people in that time and place.[1]

That's the call we have no matter where we are. No matter where our lives are located, God's call is for us to follow Jesus right here and right now, not someplace else and not later on. The novelist Wendell Berry once wrote that life is not what we wish but what we have been given.[2] That's true, isn't it? Life is not always what we wished for or hoped for, but it is what we have been given. To render it in the vernacular, "It is what it is." We are called to be faithful in the place we have been given.

Think about your location for a moment. Where are you? Are you in the middle of a troubled marriage full of tension and misunderstanding? What about work? Are you surrounded by difficult people and immersed in no-win situations? Do you get up every morning dreading the day and praying for five o'clock? How about school? Is it hard to hold on to your beliefs? Maybe you suffer from some kind of chronic physical or emotional problem. It's always there and never, ever goes away. Facing the pain every day leaves you depleted, and at times, you feel as though you're losing your soul. No, life isn't always what we wish for or hope for, but it's what we have been given. It is what it is.

Although there are no simple solutions, God's call is the same for us as it was for the church in Philippi: to live our faith where we are, no matter the shape of our circumstances. Not someplace else and later on, but right here and right now!

That's not easy, is it? Years ago, I came across Kathleen Norris's book, *Dakota*. In it, she chronicles her move with her husband from New York City to, of all places, the small town of Lemmon, South Dakota. Think of that: moving from the Big Apple to the Big Empty! From a place full of bustling energy to a place full of nothing. She insists, however, that the move was not without value. Living on the Great Plains, she says, was very much like Jacob wrestling with the angel. Life on the Great Plains demanded that she wrestle with it before it conferred a blessing.[3]

As did the Philippians before us, so too do we often have to wrestle with a place before it bestows a blessing. The places we inhabit can indeed be God's instruments in shaping and making us. Our forebears in faith had it exactly right when they spoke of this world as the "vale of soul-making." What they meant by that is simple: God uses where we are to make us.

That's not always easy to come to terms with. We don't get quick fixes and simple solutions. But the one thing we can count on is that God is faithful wherever we are. Time and again, Paul stressed this fact to the church, which was facing its share of hardship. Time and again, Paul sought to remind this congregation that no matter where they were, God was there too: "I am confident of this, that the one who began a good work among you will bring it to completion by the day of Jesus Christ" (1:6). In other words, God can be counted on to finish what he started in your life and mine. He won't let us alone until he does.

And, how about this? "And my God will fully satisfy every need of yours according to his riches in glory in Christ Jesus" (4:19). Whatever we lack for wherever we are, God can be counted on to provide.

Location, location, location. God uses where we are to make us who he wants us to become. Not someplace else and later on, but right here and right now. Right *in* the middle of where we are.

NOTES

1. Fred B. Craddock, *Philippians* (Atlanta: John Knox Press, 1985), 12.

2. Jason Peters, ed., *Wendell Berry: Life and Work* (Lexington, KY: The University of Kentucky Press, 2007), 151.

3. Kathleen Norris, *Dakota* (Boston: Houghton Mifflin Company, 1993), 1.

2

No Unfinished Business

Philippians 1:3-8

Introduction

I take a kind of perverse pleasure in cutting my yard during the spring and summer. Yes, the work is hot and sweaty, and the mower sometimes breaks down. But I enjoy the work because it is the one thing I do in the course of the week that actually gets finished. Once the grass is cut and the edges are trimmed, I can put the mower up and look over a manicured yard with enormous satisfaction. Finished! Done! At least until next week!

So much of my work as a minister is perpetually unfinished. No matter how hard I work on a sermon, it's still unfinished after I preach it. I could have said something differently. Some portions didn't work as I expected. My delivery was off. Unfinished!

The same can be said of my other weekly responsibilities. Each week I write out my "to do" list. No matter how hard I work, I never get to the end. I scratch off one item and add three more. I routinely leave my office knowing I'm just not done.

Unfinished business isn't confined to ministers, nor is it confined to work life. Most of us, at some point or other, have to cope with what we've left undone and its consequences. For example, we say hard things to someone and never get an opportunity to close the distance. Opportunities not taken shadow us with regret, leaving us wondering about what could have been. And then, there's a lot of stuff we'd love to do, but we just never get around to doing it. We rarely get to empty our "bucket list." How many of us leave this life with a lot of unfinished business?

The word that captured my attention in Philippians 1:3-8 is "completion." Paul holds out the promise that whatever God has inspired in this wonderful church will be finished. Whatever impulses they have to be faithful will not go unfulfilled. In a world where so much is incomplete, this rash promise doesn't always ring true with the people in the pews. With some, it can come off as glib, just one more example of sentimental God talk. The following sermon was my attempt to narrow the distance between the promise and its fulfillment. I also attempted to link Paul's words of long ago with the unfinished business most of us have to live with on a daily basis.

No Unfinished Business

Years ago, I was visiting a friend who lived in southern Indiana. In the course of our visit, he asked if I'd like to see several billion dollars. "Of course," I answered, "who wouldn't?" We hopped in his car and headed out of town, riding through the country until we came to a road that hadn't seen much traffic in quite a while. Turning, we continued down a tree-covered lane until we emerged in an enormous clearing. Right in front of us was the massive complex known as the Marble Hill Nuclear Power Plant. It was a tremendous facility, complete with cooling towers, buildings housing massive generators, and all kinds of control structures. Due to faulty construction and defective concrete, however, the facility would never generate a single watt of electricity. It had been deemed unsafe and so would remain forever unfinished. There's something terribly offensive about waste on that scale, especially when it's tied to something partial, something that was started but never completed.

My sense is that you and I are wired for resolution. While many of us can tolerate and even thrive in ambiguity, most of us like things to have some kind of end point. We want closure. We don't want something hanging out there in the wind. We want the checklist to be completed. When death draws close to a loved one, we want the chance to give final messages to each other, to have a last, loving conversation, to clear the air and do our best to insure we will have no regrets. We don't want to carry the unwanted and nagging load about what we should have done or should have said. Likewise, we appreciate contractors who sit down with us and go over the list of things that need to be fixed or corrected in a remodeling project. It's a relief to get them done quickly and not have to keep calling and calling and calling. We want the job done, and we want the workers out of our house so we can start living again. No, we just don't like unfinished business.

As he opened his letter to the church at Philippi, Paul offered a powerful affirmation about God's work in their lives, about God's determination to leave nothing unfinished in them and in this world: *I am confident of this, that the one who began a good work among you will bring it to completion by the day of Jesus Christ* (v. 6). In other words, God leaves nothing unfinished and nothing incomplete. There is no unfinished business. Allow me to unpack the significance of that affirmation.

God Isn't a Quitter!

The subtext of a lot of commercials is that, if we're unhappy with what we already have, we can easily find a new and better product. Don't like your car? Get a new one! Don't like your appearance? Change it! Don't like your spouse? Find a new match! Quite a few ads make their appeal by calling attention to how easy and acceptable change is. If something is not to our liking, we always have the option of walking away. If we decide that something is too difficult or too costly, we can abandon it. If our marriages present us with more challenges than we bargained for, we can walk away. No harm done! No harm to you, anyway. Some of the questions life confronts us with require too much thought or make us too uncomfortable. Better and easier to push them aside and give up on finding a solution. In these and a thousand other ways, we master the fine art of quitting. Seeing things all the way through requires tough-minded persistence, a quality sadly lacking in many of us.

But here's the good news! Paul confidently asserts that God is no quitter! He won't give up on us or on this world. In fact, that's the story all of Scripture seeks to convey. God created the world and declared it good. When we sinned, God didn't obliterate creation and start all over again; instead, he patiently and persistently worked with what God had made. That's the story behind Abraham, Isaac, and Jacob. That's the story behind Moses and the children of Israel. That's the story behind all the kings and all the prophets. And that's the story behind Jesus Christ and his church. God can't just walk away from what God made. God won't quit on us. Paul asserts that the God who was there at the beginning will be there at the end.

That affirmation is particularly potent given the fact that we live in a terribly broken world. It's certainly a world in which tragedy and chaos threaten to overwhelm us. Certainly, it was that way for the Philippians. They faced threats and persecution and wondered where their journey would end. They wondered how it would end. Paul assured them that, no matter what they faced, their lives or their struggle would not go to waste. Just so for us! God works and keeps on working—even in the aftermath of terrible events—to wrest something good and hopeful out of the raw material of our lives. The one who began a good work in you will bring it to completion. God won't quit. There is no unfinished business!

Our Incompleteness

To say that God leaves no unfinished business also calls attention to our own incompleteness. As much as Paul loved this congregation, and as much as he was grateful for their investment in his ministry, he was not blind to their shortcomings and failures. As good as they were, they weren't perfect. He saw very clearly where they had missed the mark and had gone off track. Paul hinted at this trouble when he emphasized that God would bring *to completion* what God had begun in them *by the day of Jesus Christ* (v. 6). God had started something in them, but there was still a ways to go. God had started something and would indeed finish it—but it wasn't done yet, not by a long shot.

What Paul hints at here comes into the open in the third chapter of this letter. There we read that some in the church had apparently bought into the notion that they were already perfect. Because they had received the gift of the Holy Spirit, they had no need of any further growth or development. Even more troubling, many who adopted this outlook engaged in shameful behavior, mistakenly believing that it was a sign of their spiritual maturity. Their motto was: "Because of what Jesus has done for us, we can do whatever we want." For that reason, Paul appealed to his own experience, stressing that he had not yet arrived at his utmost maturity. He still had to press on to attain the goal of his high calling in Jesus Christ. For all his experience, he wasn't there yet. By this implication, neither were the Philippians. They were good but still had some growing to do.

We can liken their difficulty to the task of working on a jigsaw puzzle. Those of you who delight in solving such puzzles know that the first step is to create the border, connecting the pieces that create the frame of the puzzle itself. Once that's done, it's all a matter of filling in the center and making a complete and coherent picture using all the pieces. That's the goal of our faith: to live in such a way that our lives present as clear a picture of Jesus Christ as possible. Some people in the Philippian church thought all they needed was the outline. But Paul stressed to them that the work is unfinished until the picture of Jesus Christ is full and complete in their lives. In fact, that's the challenge we all face: to grow and mature so that the image of Christ in us becomes clearer and less distorted.

In that light, I want to remind you that spiritual contentment is deadly: deadly for us as individual followers of Christ and deadly for us as a church. It is one thing to be at peace with one's circumstances or to have a sense that all will be well no matter what. But it is quite another to say, "Everything is fine the way it is." The One who began a good work in all of us isn't finished yet and won't be until this world comes to an end. To say God leaves nothing unfinished is to remind ourselves that *we* are nowhere near finished!

God's Work Takes Time

And finally, to declare that God leaves no unfinished business is to remind ourselves of something we chafe at: God's work in us and in this world takes time!

Unfortunately, our reading of Scripture often leaves us with the impression that all genuine work of God happens instantly. If it's of God, it happens immediately and there's no waiting! After all, Jesus healed people on the spot. Paul himself was converted in a single dramatic encounter. So we assume that if God does it, it has to happen fast. Boom! Just like that!

Paul, however, gives a longer view. God's work in us and in this world won't be completed until the *day of Jesus Christ* (v. 6). We've been waiting for that day for some two thousand years, and no one knows how much longer it will be. The only conclusion we can draw from how much time has already passed is that God isn't in a hurry.

The moving film *Amazing Grace* depicts William Wilberforce's long struggle to bring an end to the slave trade in Great Britain.[1] One scene in the film depicts young Wilberforce visiting John Newton, the former slave trader turned minister and author of the beloved hymn "Amazing Grace." Wilberforce wants Newton's advice about this undertaking, but as the conversation gets underway, Newton inquires about the state of Wilberforce's faith. He replies that he is slowly returning to it, although, in his words, "there are no lightning bolts." To which Newton replies: "God sometimes does his work with a gentle drizzle, not a storm. Drip, drip, drip."

So often, you and I view time as our enemy. It's running out, or we never have enough of it. We feel its pressure and we squeeze it hard to wrest every last drop out of it. We want things to go faster, faster, faster. And, we want God to hurry. But God is not in a hurry, and God works slowly but faithfully to bring everything—everything—to God's desired end. Drip, drip, drip.

So here's the gospel in Paul's intense but understated affirmation to his dear friends: no matter how long it takes or how slowly things unfold, God will finish what God starts. There is no unfinished business!

NOTE

1. Steven Knight, *Amazing Grace,* DVD, directed by Michael Apted (Los Angeles: Twentieth Century Fox, 2006).

Praying Life: Doing What's Best

Philippians 1:9-11

Introduction

One of the most insightful books I've come across in a long time is Robert Lupton's *Toxic Charity*. In it, Lupton argues, convincingly I think, that churches and charities often hurt the very people they intend to help. As Lupton puts it, "'good intentions' can translate into ineffective care or even harm."[1] In other words, love isn't always enough. Good intentions and charitable impulses often backfire unless those things are harnessed to a wise mind.

Paul made the same point in his opening prayer for the church at Philippi, as these alternative renderings of this week's passage make clear:

> So this is my prayer: that your love will flourish and that you will not only love much but well. Learn to love appropriately…. (The Message)

> My prayer for you is that you may have still more love—a love that is full of knowledge and wise insight. I want you to be able always to recognize the highest and the best… (Phillips Translation)

> I pray that your love will keep on growing and that you will fully know and understand how to make the right choices…. (CEV)

All of these translations forge a strong connection between love and wisdom, between love and insight. It's not enough to love; one must know how best to express that love in any given situation. Doing the right thing at the right time in the right way is not always immediately obvious.

In preparing this sermon, the connection between love and wisdom captured my attention. As followers of Christ, we know we ought to love others, especially the poor, the grieved, the isolated, the outsider. But how do we love well? That's a different story! How do we know what love requires in the moment? That's not always easy to figure out. For that reason, I decided to frame this idea the way Paul did—as a part of prayer. This is a prayer any of us could offer countless times a day: "Lord, help me to do what's best." Lord, help me to love in such a way that I help rather than hurt.

Praying Life: Doing What's Best

Love isn't always enough. Love may inspire us to act, to do something. We'll do the best thing or even the right thing. Sometimes we create near-disasters by trying to do what we deem is the "loving" thing to do. It's hard to think of love as a destructive force, but sometimes we love the wrong way. As a result, we wind up hurting rather than helping.

Case in point: Several years ago my wife Ginny and I befriended a young person who had a boatload of potential. We welcomed him into the circle of our family by treating him to meals and regularly welcoming him into our home. Over time, however, we began to realize that he came from a severely troubled background and was carrying a very heavy and destructive load of baggage. As those issues surfaced, our efforts to lend support backfired, and he began acting in ways we couldn't understand. We needed help, so we reached out to a wise and insightful counselor. He quickly identified the emotional and mental health issues this person we loved was struggling with. Then he gave us the kicker! He said, "Because of the nature of this person's problems, everything your faith tells you that you should do in this instance—be loving, caring, welcoming—everything you're doing is only making things worse." In this instance, our loving actions weren't enough; in fact they were actively unraveling the very support we were attempting to weave.

The same sort of thing happened between Paul and the church at Philippi. Of all the churches Paul started, this church loved him most. Things just clicked between the apostle and the people there, and they shared a close and intimate friendship. Naturally, when the church heard that Paul was in prison, they immediately wanted to *do* something to help him out. As they thought about the best way to help Paul, someone in the congregation suggested they send one of their own members to be a sort of personal assistant to the apostle—to look after him and take care of whatever he needed. This idea caught fire, and the church embraced it enthusiastically. After some prayer and discussion, they chose a young man named Epaphroditus to carry out the task. They quickly assembled a personalized care kit for Paul, took up a collection, and sent Epaphroditus to join Paul.

What an incredibly thoughtful gesture! This was a tremendous gift on the part of the church at Philippi. They were taking an active part in supporting Paul's ministry; that's why he called them his "partners in the gospel" (see v. 5). But their plan of action did not go well—not at all! In fact, it was a disaster that almost did Paul in! Apparently Epaphroditus wasn't ready to be away from home; he got homesick and began missing his family and friends. To make matters worse, he also became so physically ill that he nearly died! Paul wound up having to take care of the young man sent to take care of him! One of the reasons Paul wrote this letter was to thank the church for being so thoughtful. He acknowledged that sending Epaphroditus touched him greatly. But he also said to them as politely as he could, "Don't ever do that again!" The church wanted to help Paul but wound up adding to his difficulty and making his time in prison even more stressful. Love may inspire all kinds of wonderful things, but sometimes our loving actions are misguided, unwise, and unhelpful.

That truth born out of experience shows up in Paul's opening prayer for the church: *And this is my prayer, that your love may overflow more and more with knowledge and full insight to help you determine what is best...* (Philippians 1:9-10a).

Pay attention to that phrase, *to help you determine what is best.* The word for "determine" that Paul employs here is the same one used for testing coins.[2] It's all about separating the genuine from the counterfeit, the good from the bad.

Love isn't always enough; it has to be coupled with wisdom and insight. We have to figure out the best way and the right way to do the loving thing. In that light, Paul prayed for the church to have the insight to know and do what was best in any given situation.

Let's put Paul's prayer in personal terms: "Lord, help me do what's best!" That's the kind of prayer that life often forces us to make.

"Lord, help me do what's best"—that's what we pray when our lives are jumbled and confused. In today's order of service, I have included a quote from a famous philosopher. I have a copy of it on display in my study, and I look at it nearly every day:

> Lord, I have to make a choice, and I'm afraid I may make the wrong one. But I have to make it anyway, and I can't put it off. So I will make it, and trust you to forgive me if I do wrong. And Lord, I will trust You, too, to help make things right afterward.[3]

"I have to make a choice, and I'm afraid I may make the wrong one." Our choices aren't always clearly defined, nor are they simple. Our circumstances frequently give off mixed signals, making them more difficult to read and sort out. We confront too many situations where we say, "Well, on the one hand, there's this. But on the other hand, there's that." The best doesn't always announce itself, and it's not always highlighted with a neon marker. As we've seen, love doesn't always know what to do. Ask the parent of a troubled teenager. Ask the person who has to consider withdrawing life support. Ask the manager trying to make a decision, the consequences of which will affect a lot of other people. We pray, "Lord, help me do what's best" because what's best is just not always clear.

"Lord, help me do what's best." Life forces us to make that prayer because our line of sight is limited.

My car has a satellite radio, and I am addicted to it! Wherever I go, I'm never without a sports talk station or my favorite music channels. But sometimes my radio will flash the "no signal" message. A line of tall trees, a seam of towering buildings, or an imposing ridge of mountains can come between the satellite and my radio, blocking the line of sight, and I lose signal.

When we have to make a hard choice, we don't always have a clear line of sight. None of us can see as far as we'd like. We can't see around corners. We can't see over hills. None of us knows exactly how our choices will play out in the long run. The church at Philippi certainly never imagined that their plan to help Paul would turn out as badly as it did. Who can see how our actions will play out? We jump into something, and the water turns out to be far deeper than we thought. The law of unintended consequences comes into play: "I never saw that coming!" We have no idea how a choice we make is going to ripple out.

So, if we are going to pray our lives, to pray through those moments when our choices aren't at all clear, what do we do?

Exercise Imagination

Not long ago, I asked a colleague of mine to pray for me. When I had rattled off a list of three or four things I wanted prayer for, this person said, "Let's start with the first thing you mentioned. Tell me about it. Tell me why you're concerned. Give me some details, so I'll know how to pray. I want you to fill in the picture for me."

Fill in the picture. That's what I mean by exercising imagination. When we pray, "Lord, help me do what's best," we're praying that we can look *into* things and not just *at* them. We're praying we can see beneath the surface. To pray for the best means we have to think as far ahead as possible. To imagine as best we can all the different ways things will play out. To imagine how things could be, not just what they are. Lewis Smedes puts it this way: "… imagination is the inward vision of love. It's love's educated guess of what will happen to another person if we do what we think is right."[4]

Check Your Motives

Like it or not, hard choices test us. They force us to check our motives. Scripture tells us that "the heart is devious above all else; it is perverse—who can understand it?" (Jeremiah 17:9). We are layered and complex. Our faith serves us well when it helps us see ourselves as we truly are, the good and the bad. That's why praying for the best requires that we check our motives and ask ourselves what we're really wanting. After all, we have a knack for making our selfishness look virtuous! In any given situation, we can easily define "the best" only in terms of what's good for me.

Pray with Courage

Do I really want what's best if the best means I will have to make sacrifices? Do I really want what's best if it means that I will have to put up with some inconvenience or heartache? Praying, "Lord, help me do what's best" always, always bears an invitation to do some soul-searching. Do I really want what's best? Be prepared for the prayer to be turned back on you. Are you willing to do whatever it takes for the best to happen?

When it comes to praying the hard, gritty stuff of our lives, sooner or later we will discover that love isn't always enough. Even though the apostle himself extolled love as the greatest gift, he also recognized that for it to be effective, it has to be coupled with wisdom and insight. Love inspires us;

wisdom and insight guide us in doing the right thing at the right time in the right way. When we harness our loving intention to thoughtful reflection, we stand a far better chance of doing the best thing and not making things worse.

NOTES

1. Robert D. Lupton, *Toxic Charity* (New York: HarperOne, 2011), 2.

2. The word Paul employs here is δοκιμαζειν See R. P. Martin, *The Epistle of Paul to the Philippians* (Grand Rapids: Eerdmans, 1959), 65-66.

3. Attributed to Søren Kierkegaard.

4. Lewis B. Smedes, *Choices: Making Right Decisions in a Complex World* (San Francisco: HarperSanFranciso, 1986), 111.

4

Interpreting My Chains

Philippians 1:12-18

Introduction

Human beings are essentially "meaning makers." We instinctively look for connections and patterns. As we age, we question if what we have done with our days has had any significance. Deep down, I imagine all of us hope that our lives can't be reduced to mere chance or a random accident. We want our lives to add up to more than the sum of the years we have taken up space on the planet.

As a result, I think most people strive in some sort of way to interpret their lives, to read between the lines of events and to look more deeply into their circumstances, to find something that suggests there's more to life than we can see. Yes, we sometimes look back with regret, grieving over what might have been if we had made a different choice. But we also look back, intently searching for connections between something that happened back there and how it affected where we are now. We also try to make sense of present circumstances. How did we get here? Is this the way it will always be? Why this and why now? Unlike scientists who are striving to develop a "Grand Unified Theory" that explains absolutely everything, our aims are much smaller. We are less interested in the meaning of all life than we are the meaning *in* our lives.

Paul speaks to our search for significance. Like Paul, all of us are bound to something. We are chained to things, some good and some bad. The trick for all of us is to figure out what those chains mean. Hearing their daily rattle, we want very much to know if we're reading them right and if they are serving some good purpose. In the final analysis, we all seek to "interpret our chains."

Interpreting my Chains

I brought a length of chain with me this morning. There's really nothing extraordinary about several feet of good, strong chain, the kind available at any hardware store. A length of chain can come in handy for all kinds of jobs. It's a useful item to have in the back of the truck when we want to yank something out of the ground. Maybe a length of chain is just what we need to repair a child's swing set. When Ginny and I got married, our very first purchase together was a washer and dryer. (How romantic can you get?) We went to an appliance store, and the salesperson took a length of chain like this and threw it into the drum of the dryer several times. The chain never dented or scratched the drum. We bought that very model, and the piece of chain sold us! A length of chain has all kinds of uses.

But our minds move in an entirely different direction when we think about a length of chain being used to bind and shackle someone's ankles. We get a different picture if we imagine this length of chain being manacled around someone's neck. We immediately think "prisoner". We immediately think "slave". We immediately think "loss of freedom".

Paul was in chains, bound and held fast by all the power of the Roman Empire. His future was in question. He had no idea whether he would be set free or sentenced to death. The church at Philippi had gotten word of his imprisonment, and they were anxious about his welfare. They were worried sick about his ability to endure the physical rigors and hardships of a Roman jail. After all, one of the converts in the Philippian church was a jailer himself! He knew firsthand the torment that chains inflict upon a person. The church had good reason to worry about their friend.

But, if we read between the lines of this part of the letter, we can hear the unspoken question the church was asking Paul: where is God in this for you? What is the connection between your chains and the work of God? In this brief portion of the letter, Paul sought to "interpret his chains."[1] By reflecting on the apostle's response to his adversity, you and I can gain some needed and necessary wisdom for interpreting the course of our lives.

Our First Conclusions Are Not Always Right

I'm sure prison was the last place Paul wished to be. He'd been imprisoned before, so he was accustomed to the hardships of incarceration. Nevertheless, for someone possessed of such a strong sense of mission, I'm certain Paul considered it an unwanted detour and perhaps even a waste of valuable time. Given his volatile temperament, he was likely frustrated: "God, what am I doing *in* here? If I were *out* there, there's no telling how many people I could reach! You called me to preach—why on earth am I locked up? This just doesn't make sense! You got me out of jail before—why not now?" The worst punishment for someone who is driven to accomplish something is to be deprived of an opportunity, and that's where Paul was. All the way around, this whole situation just looked like a bad deal.

The truth, however, is that our judgments about where we are and what's happening to us are extremely limited. We just don't know enough or see enough to make an immediate determination about the events that overtake us. This truth is wonderfully apparent in an archetypal Chinese story about a man and his horse.[2] As the story goes, a farmer had a single horse on which he depended for everything, from pulling the plow to getting him from place to place. One day a bee stung his horse, and the horse ran off into the mountains. The old farmer searched and searched but never found the horse. His friends and neighbors came to console him, all telling him what bad luck it was that he had lost his horse. The old man responded: "Bad luck, good luck—who is to say?"

A week later the old farmer's horse returned on its own with twelve wild horses in tow. The farmer corralled these animals and was delighted at his windfall. His neighbors came by again, this time to congratulate him on his good fortune. Once again, he responded: "Bad luck, good luck—who is to say?"

The old farmer and his son attempted to break the wild horses so they could be sold. But, as the son tried to do this, one of the horses threw him, and he broke his leg in three places. As before, word spread, and his friends and neighbors came by to lament his son's injury and his terrible misfortune. And, again he said, "Bad luck, good luck—who is to say?"

Two weeks later, war broke out in some of the provinces, and the army came through the little village conscripting every able-bodied male under fifty. Because the son was injured, he didn't have to go. It turned out his broken leg saved his life, for everyone who had been drafted was killed in the fighting. "Bad luck, good luck—who is to say?"

Paul wrote to assure the church they mustn't be worried about him or his mission. The inward reality of his imprisonment was very different from its outward appearance. Paul told them that his circumstances, as bad as they were, had in fact resulted in the advance of the gospel. Paul's assessment of his imprisonment when he wrote this letter was vastly different than when he started his ministry.

The lesson holds for us. We just don't know enough at first to pass final judgment on where we are and what's happening. Like Paul, when we seek to interpret our chains and our circumstances, we have to acknowledge that our first take on what's going on may not be the whole story. In God's hands—well, God is endlessly creative and full of surprises.

Measure Where We Are Against What Matters

One of the more striking features of this portion of Paul's letter is the fact that although the church was desperate to hear how *he* was doing, the first thing he told them was how the *gospel* was doing. Although they were anxious for some scrap of information about how he was holding up, the Apostle said nary a word about himself. In fact, this portion of the letter almost crackles with energy and excitement as Paul relayed to his friends the wonderful news that although he was chained, the gospel wasn't. Although he was bound, God wasn't. As a result of his imprisonment, others had stepped into the gap and had begun to preach with great boldness and confidence. It's clear from his writing that all Paul cared about was the gospel.

In that light, do you hear what he left *unsaid*? By emphasizing the progress of the gospel, his unspoken message was this: "My circumstances don't matter! What has happened to me is of little consequence. The only thing that matters is the proclamation of the good news of Jesus Christ." That's the subtext here. What's going on here is that Paul had determined to measure where he was and what had happening to him against the larger and more important purpose of his life. As a result, he was able to see beyond his chains. Remember what he prayed at the opening of this letter? He prayed that the church would grow in knowledge and insight so they could understand…what? "What really counts!" Here, Paul showed them what an answer to that prayer looked like. The apostle was able to get a handle on where he was because he carried a well-cultivated sense of what was truly important. He had connected his chains to a larger purpose and thus was able to make sense of where he was.

That's vital. Viktor Frankl, the renowned author and psychiatrist, was one of those consigned to the living hell of Auschwitz. He survived, and his reflection on his experience there is never far from the surface of many of his writings. In one of his books, he describes at great length the psychic condition of those who were imprisoned as he was, chronicling the mental journey most of them made. He said that many prisoners eventually despaired of everything and lost their sense of the future. There was nothing to look forward to. As a result, life had no meaning, and they were thus overcome with a debilitating sense of apathy.[3] Their lives didn't matter, and death didn't matter either. So, they gave up.

That thought process highlights something of Paul's own experience and ours. You see, we can endure an awful lot if we believe it matters. If our struggle and suffering appear random and arbitrary, they will draw the life right out of us, leaving us hollow and empty. Life is reduced to going through the motions. But if we can measure our pains against some larger reason, against something that matters, then we can endure. When you and I seek to interpret our chains, to make sense of where we are, Paul's experience calls us to keep looking for ways in which our struggles serve our larger purpose.

Every Place and Every Circumstance Can Be Salvaged

I think it's important that, as Paul briefed the Philippians on how things were working out, he didn't say that God had put him in prison. Nor did he allude to some divine master plan governing every aspect and detail of his life. What he does say was this: where he is, bad as it is, God is at work *right there*. Paul discovered that although he was in chains, the gospel itself could not be chained. Although he was bound, God was not. Prison became his pulpit. God salvaged a tough place and turned it into a means by which the gospel could be advanced.

As we seek to wrest some significance and meaning from our circumstances, it's vital that we hold fast to the notion that God can work anywhere and everywhere. Any place, no matter how difficult, can be turned so that it serves God's good purpose.

Do you remember the story of Joseph from the book of Genesis? Joseph's brothers hated him because he was their father's favorite. They hated him because he was a snitch and a tattle-tale. They hated him because he persisted in telling them his crazy dreams about the day when they would have to look up to him. They attempted to get rid of Joseph by selling him into slavery. Joseph wound up in Egypt. Despite many setbacks, Joseph eventually rose to a place of prominence and power. A famine forced Joseph's brothers to travel to Egypt in search of food, and eventually, they met up with their long-lost brother. In a moment of high drama, Joseph revealed himself to his brothers, who were terrified that their brother would take revenge on them. Joseph, however, welcomed and embraced them, telling them that God had used his misfortune to save their lives: "You intended to do harm to me, God intended it for good" (Genesis 50:20). In other words, God had turned their evil into the very means by which Joseph was able to save their lives.

That's what Paul's chains communicate. Even our worst places and predicaments are not beyond God's reach. God is always at work, and God is always at work *everywhere.*

What do you see in your chains? What do you make of the circumstances that hold you fast? Paul reminds us that there's more to our chains than we know. And, indeed, they may be the means by which God does his very, very best work!

NOTES

1. Fred B. Craddock, *Philippians* (Atlanta: John Knox Press, 1985), 24.
2. John R. Claypool, "Good Luck, Bad Luck—Who Is to Say?" *The Library of Distinctive Sermons*, vol. 1, ed. Gary W. Kingsporn (Sisters, OR: Questar Publishers, 1996), 31-32.
3. Viktor E. Frankl, *The Doctor and the Soul* (New York: Alfred A. Knopf, 1960), 109ff.

Thinking Out Loud

Philippians 1:19-26

Introduction

To live is to decide. Our ability to make choices is one of the most marvelous and frightening things we shoulder. We are constantly making decisions. Bacon and eggs for breakfast or oatmeal? Does this tie go with this suit? This car or that one? This preschool or that one? Should I accept this new job offer or stay put? We make decisions all the time, and some are of little consequence while others will play out for the rest of our days.

The big decisions keep us up at night. We list the pros and cons on a legal pad. We try to free ourselves of space and time and project ourselves into the future to see how a choice might play out. We gather as much information as we possibly can to map the terrain a decision might lead us into. We pay attention to what our gut is telling us, whether it's setting off alarm bells or giving us a "go" signal. One of the bits of wisdom that has been handed down for generations is this: we just never know. For all our effort, we never really know for sure how a decision will play itself out.

Still, one of the best strategies we can pursue when making a tough call is to talk it through with a trusted friend. Letting someone else in on our thought process often clarifies our own conclusions. Talking it out uncovers the heart. In addition, talking and thinking out loud gives that trusted friend the opportunity to speak some truth into us. They can help us identify the flaws in our reasoning, encourage us when our gifts and the opportunity seem to match, and point out alternatives we've missed. In such instances, the best gift a good friend can offer us is a listening ear.

In this text, we overhear Paul as he thinks "out loud" and weighs his options for the future. Although his ultimate fate is out of his hands, he does try to come to terms with the possibilities his potential options might bring. He honors his friendship with the Philippian church by opening his heart to them. The discipline of genuine Christian friendship is on display here as the church offers Paul the gift of a listening ear.

Thinking Out Loud

Here's a typical experience. A friend calls and invites you to meet for coffee. You agree, and as soon as you arrive at the coffee house, you notice your friend appears terribly agitated and anxious. After the customary exchange of pleasantries, your friend confides that she is facing a really tough decision, one that presents no clear-cut alternative. There is no bright line marking out the best path. For the moment, all your friend asks of you is simply to listen. She needs someone else to hear her talk things through out loud—not to decide for her but to help her clarify her options and their possible consequences.

I have no doubt nearly everyone here this morning has relied on a friend for the same kind of support. Indeed, one of the best gifts we can give one another is the freedom to think out loud. To give someone some space to weigh their options and to be honest about their struggles. A true friend listens not just for the pluses and minuses of a particular decision; she listens for the soul, for what's inside us. We're at our best as the body of Christ when we allow others to think out loud and when we hold their words gently, thoughtfully, and carefully.

Paul paid that high compliment to the church at Philippi, and at this juncture in his letter, we catch the apostle thinking out loud and sharing as honestly as he knew how about his fate and his future. To his closest friends, he laid out how he saw the rest of his life unfolding, trusting them to pray on his behalf as he faced an uncertain future and a conflicting choice.

The stakes were high for Paul: nothing less than life or death. Paul faced some very real and very stark alternatives. As he saw it, he could either be released from prison and have the opportunity to further his ministry, or he could be executed by the state. Every day he felt the weight of his chains, and every day he knew the frustration of not being able to fulfill his calling. And every day he knew he just might be one step closer to death. Paul didn't try to muster up some false bravado, nor did he try to act as if nothing mattered. Not by a long shot! In fact, the intensity of his struggle is very much out in the open in this portion of the letter.

Here's an instance where our English translations are much smoother than the original. In the original language, the syntax of these verses is broken, irregular, and disjointed, and it mirrors the turbulence in Paul's own mind.[1] In addition, Paul's troubled state becomes obvious by the way he acts as if it's all up to him—as if the choice were entirely in his hands. That's how we react, isn't it? Even though something is clearly beyond our control, we persist in focusing on what *we* need to do. Everything here highlights the fact that the apostle was terribly uncertain about what lay ahead.

So, as best he could, Paul attempted to sort out his options. When I read these verses, I get a mental picture of Paul doing what we do whenever we're facing a similar dilemma. We take out a sheet of paper, draw a line right down the center, and list the pros on one side and the cons on the other. For Paul, the list might look something like this:

As Paul saw it, the choice was nothing less than one between life and

Life	Death
For me it is Christ.	It is gain
If I live on, there is fruitful labor.	to be with Christ.
Pastoral responsibility demands my continuing presence.	

death. As he played with his options, he could see the positives on both sides. Life and death were just about equal. No wonder, then, that he told the Philippians that he was *hard pressed between the two* (v. 23). That word presents a picture of a traveler walking down a path that becomes narrower and narrower and narrower until he is hemmed in and can't move from one side to the other.[2] Paul was hemmed in, squeezed on both sides. He was pulled in two different directions, gripped by uncertainty and indecision. What would really be best? It was a hard call.

Jesus himself faced such a decision early in his ministry (Mark 1:35-39). According to Mark, Jesus initially enjoyed tremendous success in and around the village of Capernaum. He was casting out demons, healing the sick, and preaching. Word spread, and his reputation grew. His disciples even said to him, "Everyone is searching for you" (v. 37). It would have been easy for Jesus to remain right where he was and let everyone come to him. But Jesus was grasped by a larger mission and felt restless. Should he stay or should he go on to other places? The decision weighed on him so heavily that he spent an entire night in prayer, trying to sort out his next move with God. Make no mistake about it—Jesus was hard pressed.

And, so was Paul. Hard pressed. Squeezed. Hemmed in and uncertain about the future.

Although Paul's uncertainty and anxiety leak out profusely, he does manage to hold on to one overriding conviction: *...for I know that through your prayers and the help of the Spirit of Jesus Christ this will turn out for my deliverance.* (Philippians 1:19).

"This will be my salvation." That's a direct quote from the book of Job (13:16). Job, you may recall, went through a world of hurt. He suffered the loss of his family and his possessions. He was afflicted with terrible physical suffering. His friends despised him; they gave up on him and assumed the worst about him. Despite all that, Job voiced his confidence that God would indeed vindicate him. God's justice would eventually be served, and Job would indeed be declared innocent.

So, sitting in a Roman jail, shackled hand and foot, suffering all manner of deprivation, wondering whether each day would be his last, Paul defiantly shouts, "This—no matter what happens—*this* will turn out for my deliverance! If I strike the tent of this mortal body, that is gain because I will be with Christ. And, if I live, that's good, too, because there is something I can do—there is fruitful labor yet remaining for me. If you keep praying for me and the Spirit keeps supplying my needs, whatever happens, I just can't lose!"

"Whatever happens, I can't lose!" What a powerful affirmation about the presence and work of God in our lives. How in the world could Paul say that? How in the world could you or I ever say that?

Years ago, I came across a description of God as a chess master.[3] Now I don't know anything at all about chess, but as I understand it, the possibilities become astronomical after the first few moves. The best chess masters are able to anticipate and respond to the infinite range of possible moves. In the same way, God can and does respond to the infinite range of our choices. He can even take our wrong choices into account! Whatever move we make, God is able to meet us right there. Wherever we go, God is right there waiting for us, working to turn our choices into something hopeful and positive. "I am absolutely certain that this will turn out for my deliverance. Whatever happens, I can't lose!"

Perhaps you are in a place today that requires a little thinking out loud. Like Paul, you are hard pressed. You are pulled in two different directions at once. You have no idea what's going to unfold or how life is going to sort itself out. Maybe the pressure is so intense, all you can do is shout, "I just don't know what to do!"

Lord, I'm hard pressed! I don't know whether to keep my job or move on.

Lord, I'm hard pressed! Do I go through the treatment or just let go?

Lord, I'm hard pressed! No matter what I do here, somebody's going to get hurt!

Lord, I'm hard pressed! I don't know what to do to help my children!

Lord, I'm hard pressed! I just don't have any good options. I don't have any clear alternatives.

If that's you, follow Paul's lead! Think out loud. Lean on someone here. Talk with a friend. Speak as honestly as you know how to the Almighty. Talk out loud until you grab hold of a choice.

But remember, whatever you and I choose, whatever comes, "this will turn out for *our* deliverance!" God will be there on the other side of our choices, no matter what. And, because of that, you and I, just like Paul—well, we just can't lose!

NOTES

1. David E. Garland, "The Defense and Confirmation of the Gospel," *Review and Expositor* (Summer, 1980), 334.

2. Marvin R. Vincent, *Philippians and Philemon*, ICC (Edinburgh: T & T Clark, 1897), 28; R. P. Martin, *The Epistle of Paul to the Philippians* (Grand Rapids: Eerdmans, 1959), 78.

3. E. Glenn Hinson, *A Serious Call to a Contemplative Lifestyle* (Philadelphia: The Westminster Press, 1974), 45.

Worthy of the Gospel

Philippians 1:27-30

Introduction

Commercial flight has lost the glamour it once had. Not only are ticket prices up, so are the inconveniences. One of the most obvious examples of this reality shows up whenever we attempt to check in for our flight and find that one of our bags is over the weight limit. On countless occasions, I have witnessed people pulling stuff out of their luggage and either tucking it into another bag or simply handing it off to a relative or friend. I have seen the wheels turning in their minds. They seem to be asking themselves, "What's essential? What do I really need? What can I do without?" The exercise is important; those extra pounds of stuff are costly and no one wants to pay extra.

I wrote this sermon with a lively awareness that most people are overloaded. Their lives are "over the limit" in terms of competing obligations and unceasing pressure. We have a lot to carry and a lot to keep up with. We rarely think about paring life down; instead, we think about adding more and more.

But the danger of overloading our lives is that we stand to lose sight of that which is most important and most critical. The environment and culture we inhabit possess enormous power to warp the soul and make us less than we were meant to be. Jesus had it right when he said that we can "possess everything and still lose our souls" (Matthew 6:26).

For this reason, I was drawn to Paul's emphatic instruction to the church: Only live worthy of the gospel (Philippians 1:27). "Only" is an important word. It insists that priorities and essentials move to the head of the line. It insists that we make every effort to travel light and leave behind the excess baggage of trivial commitments.

Worthy of the Gospel

Most of us, I'm sure, can remember a teacher who exerted a great deal of influence over our lives. That teacher may have seen we were heading in the wrong direction, and somehow he or she got our attention and got us back on the right track. Others made a difference because they saw and nurtured potential that we didn't know we had. They believed in us and urged us to dream big dreams. Still other teachers influenced us because of the ideas they presented and the skills they exhibited in the art of teaching itself.

One of my former teachers, Dr. Frank Stagg, falls into that latter category. Dr. Stagg was a wonderful gentleman and a keen New Testament scholar. He expected the best from his students, just as he expected the best from himself. One of the ideas I heard Dr. Stagg present was his notion that "salvation was both gift and demand."[1] By that, Dr. Stagg insisted that our salvation was first and foremost a gift of God, not attainable by human effort or achievement. We are saved by God's grace and God's grace alone. Nevertheless, Dr. Stagg also insisted that salvation brings with it a very clear demand. It requires everything of us. Faith is not merely a matter of the heart; it has to be translated into daily living. The grace of God is free, yet it demands all we are and all we have.

You may have noticed that, in all Paul's writings, he frequently emphasized the demand side of faith. He couldn't help himself! Sooner or later, he reached for imperatives and started issuing commands, telling the recipients of his letters what they must *do*. So here, at this juncture in Philippians, Paul once again turned to the situation facing the church and reminded them of the demand side of the divine equation of God's grace. We catch it right off the bat with the very first word in this section: "only." *Only!* It's emphatic. Only live worthy of the gospel of Jesus Christ. Whatever else we're about, remember to live worthy of the gospel. Whatever else is going on, remember this is most important. No matter whatever else we have to do, do this one thing. *Only* live worthy of the gospel. Paul said to the church in Philippi, "Conduct yourselves in a manner worthy of the gospel, one that reflects that you are first and foremost a citizen, not of Rome, but of the Kingdom of God" (v. 27).[2] By means of this imperative, Paul emphasized the demand side of the gospel ledger.

That imperative was no doubt a timely reminder for the church at Philippi, given the ways in which their faith was being tested. And, it is equally timely for us.

For one, the church wasn't at all sure Paul would be around to help them. Although the apostle had confidently asserted in the previous verses his conviction that he would be released from prison, here he is more cautious. A bit unsure. Ever the realist, Paul didn't want them to get their hopes up too high, and so he took pains to remind them that things might not work out as they, and he, hoped. His future was still up in the air, and Paul wanted to soften the blow if things didn't work out. More importantly, he wanted them to understand they might have to face their next challenges without his help and support. They would be on their own. In that light, the Philippians' faith must not be tied to Paul but to Christ. They had to own their faith for themselves. So, Paul stressed to them: "Whether I'm there or not, the important thing is for you to keep living out the gospel of Jesus Christ."

The hard truth is that, for too many of us, our faith is thin. Put us in a hard place, remove the things we depend on to prop ourselves up, or leave us utterly alone, and the veneer of our faith quickly peels off. The theologian Langdon Gilkey captured this truth in his memoir of his experience in a Japanese internment camp during World War II, entitled *Shantung Compound*. As Gilkey relates it, two thousand men, women, and children were herded into a camp and forced to live a marginal existence. Sadly, the conditions they endured stripped away all pretense and quickly revealed each person's true character.[3] Some people, assumed at the start of their captivity to be really good people, became the most selfish. Without structures to prop up their goodness, their character quickly eroded, and they gave in to their baser instincts. In the same vein, a national newspaper did a story on business travel and described how easy and common it is for business travelers to ignore their marital commitments while away from home. They assume time and distance provide a layer of security. They would never be found out, and their actions could be neatly compartmentalized. They live by that popular adage: "What happens in Vegas, stays in Vegas!"

What would *you* do if no one were looking? What would you do if you knew you wouldn't be caught? In this light, Paul's admonition for the church to live in a manner worthy of the gospel whether he was present or absent bears a call for us to cultivate a faith that is consistent no matter where we are or what the circumstances.

Furthermore, the church was in danger of being *intimidated by [their] opponents* (v. 28). Paul's choice of words here is very descriptive, and the word paints a picture of a band of horses, spooked, and stampeding in all directions. From its beginning, the church at Philippi faced hostility and opposition. And, since Paul's departure and his subsequent imprisonment, things had only gotten worse. Paul feared the adversity would eventually get the best of them, leading them to cave to the pressure.

During his journey to the cross, Jesus possessed enormous ego integrity. Time and again, he refused to be swayed by popular enthusiasm. Time and again, he refused the crowd's efforts to mold him into their kind of king. Even while hanging on the cross, he endured one last temptation hurled at him by his adversaries. They urged him to "come down from the cross" and demonstrate once and for all that he was indeed the Son of God (Mark 15:30). But Jesus knew that the only way to prove that he was indeed God's own Son was not to come down but to stay up there. And he resisted with all of his might and all his strength the urge to give in to the pressure, to be stampeded by the demands of others.

I have an idea our faith is tested in the same sort of way. Years ago, I came across a letter a missionary had written to Carlyle Marney, the Baptist preacher of a generation ago. In that letter, this missionary chronicled some of the difficulties and struggles he faced doing his work on a far-flung mission field. The most difficult challenge, he said was to learn "to walk without being shoved."[4] To walk without being shoved. That's so us. Live worthy of the gospel. Don't allow yourself to get stampeded. Don't let yourself be shoved. Don't panic. Hang tough—even if there are more of them than there are of us.

The final test this church faced was suffering. Paul commented that the Philippians were facing the same sort of struggle he himself had already endured. The hostility and adversity—not to mention the threat of imprisonment—they face was because they were followers of Jesus Christ. No other reason. Few things possess greater capacity to diminish our humanity and uproot our faith than suffering, no matter what form it takes. By its very nature, suffering means to be "acted upon" by someone or something. Our lives and our circumstances are beyond our control. We are helpless and powerless. It is a brute fact, a hard reality to be avoided at all costs.

Paul, however, had a different take on suffering. Notice how he put it: *For he has graciously granted you the privilege not only of believing in Christ, but of suffering for him as well* (v. 29). That's not a perspective you and I hear much today, is it? The predominant proclamation of the gospel in our time is actually a perversion of it: health and wealth. Believe and be rich. Believe and be successful. Believe and get whatever you want. That's a far cry from *you [have] the privilege not only of believing in [him], but of suffering for him as well* isn't it? Paul's wording is terribly important. He describes it as a gift of grace.

Suffering, terrible as it is, can be a means of grace and a means of bearing witness. I know of no more powerful witness than those in the church who confront suffering on a daily basis and keep their faith whole and intact. Whether it be chronic pain, a hostile environment, or marginalization, those who embrace suffering and hold on to their faith—who become enlarged rather than diminished by it—are the real saints in my book. Even in the face of suffering, they have determined to live in a manner worthy of the gospel of Jesus Christ. Such is indeed the clearest imitation of Christ's example.

What tests are you facing today? What out there or in here is pressing on you? A temptation to unhook your life from your commitment? The never-ending pressure to just ride the status quo? Pain, suffering, heartache, difficulty? Make no mistake about it: the gospel places demands upon us. It requires everything we've got. Whatever life brings, our calling is to live in such a way that we reflect the truth and power of the gospel of Jesus Christ. Remember, living worthy of the gospel is the *only* thing that matters!

NOTES

1. Frank Stagg, *Polarities of Human Existence in Biblical Perspective* (Macon, GA: Smyth & Helwys, 1994), 149ff.

2. The verb Paul employed here, πολιτεύεσθε, conveys the idea of citizenship, a concept the Philippians would have understood well.

3. Langdon Gilkey, *Shantung Compound* (San Francisco: Harper and Row, 1966), 92.

4. Carlyle Marney, *Achieving Family Togetherness* (Nashville: Abingdon Press, 1958), 110-111.

7

Get Your Mind Right!

Philippians 2:1-4

Introduction

Assumptions possess enormous power. If we anticipate that a meeting will be heated and contentious, we will likely enter ready to do battle, with all our arguments and counterarguments lined out and locked and loaded. If we assume another person is at fault for some lapse or failure, then we will engage the conversation more as prosecutors than as friends. Our assumptions inform our behavior. We tend to act on what we think. Our frame of mind often writes the script we will follow in our interactions.

We would be shortsighted, however, if we limited this insight to negative behavior. The truth is, how we think can encourage us to behave in a positive and constructive manner. In this particular instance, Paul chose to influence the Philippians' behavior positively by reminding them of who they were and what they had already experienced instead of chastising them for who they weren't. In the book and film *The Help*, the maid Aibileen encourages the young girl who she helped raise with the repeated refrain, "You is kind, you is smart, you is important."[1] Aibileen was attempting to tell this child who she was rather than pointing out what she wasn't.

Perhaps we would do well as individual followers of Christ and as gathered congregations if we were regularly reminded of who we are in Christ instead of being scolded for who we are not. If we would spend more time thinking about what we have received from Christ and experienced together, we would likely come closer to realizing the unity and togetherness Paul spoke of in these verses. If we regularly called each other kind, smart, and important, we would be more likely to act that way and so reflect "the mind of Christ" (1 Corinthians 2:16).

Get Your Mind Right!

Let's begin with three seemingly unrelated items:

Do you remember the children's story *The Little Engine That Could*? It's an inspirational tale about a little switch engine that took on the task of pulling a long train of railroad cars over an extraordinarily long and steep mountain. The task was so daunting that other, more powerful engines refused. But this little switch engine embraced the challenge and went puffing up the mountain, telling itself over and over, "I think I can, I think I can, I think I can." And as you know, the engine made it.

Item number two. Some years ago, I caught a documentary about the Blue Angels, the Navy's aerobatic team, on TV. When they perform, they do some incredible maneuvers and some very precise formation flying—really amazing stuff. Interestingly enough, however, the documentary showed how the pilots practiced their routines *on the ground*. Before an air show, they gather together in a room and sit down. Every pilot closes his eyes, and then the commander of the group calls out all the instructions for every maneuver and every routine, from takeoff to landing and everything in-between. In other words, they fly the entire show before they ever take off.

Item number three. If we're involved in a serious conversation or negotiation with another person, what we think about that person can make all the difference in the process. Is that individual an enemy or a friend? Do we see them as an adversary or an ally? Can I trust them, or do I need to have my guard up? My assumptions about that other person will affect how I handle my end of the bargain and how I approach the conversation.

Those three examples call attention to the powerful connection between what we think and what we do. The power of the mind to influence our actions and behavior is enormous.

This assumption informed Paul's approach to one of the problems facing the church at Philippi. As I've mentioned before, Paul recognized that the church, for all its strengths, was under a great deal of pressure from without and from within.[2] They had to figure out how to live their faith in a hostile environment with the looming threat of continued persecution. As often happened in Paul's ministry, his adversaries showed up, trying to undermine his influence and wean followers away from the gospel. If that wasn't enough, there were some serious disagreements between members that had boiled over into the life of the entire church. As a result, the problems of a few became everybody's problems, and people were beginning to take sides. Add all that up, and we can see that the church was under an enormous strain, and the glue holding the congregation together was cracking.

Up to this point, Paul had only hinted at this trouble indirectly, but here he brought it out in the open and addressed it directly. He engaged in some long-distance crisis management, doing what he could from the confines of a Roman jail to help them stick together despite the forces threatening to pull them apart.

In that light, notice how Paul proceeded and note the strategy he employed. In particular, pay attention to the tone he employed in these verses. Most of us assume, I think, that if Paul needed to get the members of this church in line, he would have issued some stern commands and thundered at them. One of the more interesting peculiarities I have noticed about church members over the years is that sometimes we feel good about worship only after we've been made to feel bad. "How was church?" "Great! The sermon really stepped on my toes! It reminded me what a miserable wretch I am!" If we feel really guilty, then our faith must be okay. Although I wonder what that says about us, this approach points to the fact that we sometimes have to confront some uncomfortable truths head-on, and subtlety just won't get the job done. In light of the seriousness of the threat to the Philippian church, I think we would have expected Paul to lay out their shortcomings and failures in no uncertain terms, letting them have it with both barrels: Shape up! Get your act together! Paul would have been in character if he had done that. After all, he was never timid about speaking his mind, sometimes in very harsh tones and with rough language. (The letters to the churches in Galatia and Corinth come to mind. Paul certainly didn't pull any punches with them!)

Still, that wasn't Paul's approach here. Instead of highlighting their deficiencies and weaknesses, he called attention to the things they had in common: *If then there is any encouragement in Christ, any consolation from love, any sharing in the Spirit, any compassion and sympathy* (2:1). Most of our English translations render this verse in such a way as to cast doubt that the things Paul speaks of here are real. If! A better way to render it is "If then there is any encouragement in Christ—and there is!" "If there is any consolation from love—and there is!" "If there is any sharing in the Spirit—and there is!" "If there is any compassion and sympathy—and there is!"[3] That puts this verse in a whole different light, doesn't it? In this way, then, Paul appealed to what the church had already experienced together. They already knew what it was to be called and encouraged by Christ.

They had already experienced the comfort that love for one another could provide. They had already shared in the power and presence of the Holy Spirit. They had already been on the receiving end of mercy and kindness from one another. As Paul saw it, the Philippians had too much shared experience to give up on one another now. It's as if Paul was saying to them, "Whatever the problems you are encountering, the resources you already have in Jesus Christ are more than adequate. You have far more to hold you together than there is to drive you apart."

Instead of punishing them with a guilt trip, Paul called on them to remember who they were and what they already had. He reminded them that their greatest resource was who they were and what they already knew.[4] In other words, he called on them to recalibrate their thinking by focusing on what they had in common. The first step in resolving their difficulties was to get their minds right by focusing, not on their troubles but on the resources they already possessed. Get your mind right by remembering who you are, that you are "in Christ." Do that, and everything else will take care of itself.

Years ago, William Willimon wrote about a birthday party thrown for a little boy in his neighborhood. His name was Clayton, and for his fourth birthday his mother told him he could have any kind of party he wanted.

> "I want a party where everybody there will be kings and queens," Clayton replied without a moment's hesitation. His wish was granted.
>
> His mother started to work, creating a score of golden paper crowns, royal blue crepe paper robes with gold lining, and scepters made from coat hangers and cardboard. Then the afternoon of the party came. As the guests arrived, they were delighted to receive royal crowns, robes, and scepters. Everyone at the party was either a king or queen. And everyone had a wonderful time at Clayton's party. All the guests enjoyed cake and ice cream. They had a majestic procession up to the end of the block and back. All looked like kings and queens. All believed they were kings and queens. Moreover they all *acted* like kings and queens. They all behaved in a most regal manner.[5]

That little story captures the point. Dress up like who we are and we will act like it. Remember who we are and what we already have, then we will do the right thing. Think rightly and we will behave rightly, often taking care of our problems.

Get your thinking right, remembering that all our brothers and sisters are already kings and queens in God's eyes, and we will *do nothing from selfish ambition or conceit* (2:3).

Get your mind right, remembering that you and I are a "royal priesthood," and we will find it easier to *regard others as better than yourselves* and to look out for their interests as well as our own (1 Peter 2:9; Philippians 2:3).

Get your mind right, remembering that together we have heard Christ call us by name and have felt him come alongside us in our joys and sorrows, remembering how we have been consoled and comforted by divine love, remembering how powerfully we have experienced the Holy Spirit, and remembering how deeply we cared for one another in the beginning.

Get your thinking right, remembering who we are and where we have been, and we will find we have more than enough to meet the challenges that threaten to pull us apart.

What we think influences how we live. Our attitudes get translated into behavior. Get your mind right. Remember what we have in common, and we will stand a better chance of staying together no matter what comes our way.

NOTES

1. Kathryn Stockett, *The Help* (New York: Penguin Random House, 2009).

2. A good overview of the context of this letter may be found in Frank Stagg, "Philippians," *The Broadman Bible Commentary*, vol. 11 (Nashville: Broadman Press, 1971), 182-183; and Fred B. Craddock, *Philippians* (Atlanta: John Knox Press, 1985), 36-37.

3. R. P. Martin, *The Epistle of Paul to the Philippians* (Grand Rapids: Eerdmans, 1959), 90.

4. Craddock, *Philippians*, 36.

5. William H. Willimon, *The Gospel for the Person Who Has Everything* (Valley Forge: Judson Press, 1978), 76.

Climbing Down the Ladder

Philippians 2:5-11

Introduction

Of late, a key topic in national conversation has been the stagnation of lower and middle class wages and salaries. This is indeed a matter of great consequence and importance because one of the building blocks of the American dream has been that hard work results in upward mobility. If we work hard, we'll be rewarded with increases in pay and more opportunities. By working hard, we can "climb the ladder" and "get to the top." We can rise as high as our work and abilities can take us.

Paul's "hymn to Christ" in Philippians 2:5-11 calls attention to Jesus' willingness to move down rather than up. Instead of climbing up the ladder, Jesus climbed down in order to identify with us. Jesus, it seems, embraced "downward mobility" for our sake. Paul held up Jesus' humility in this regard as a corrective to those in the church who apparently were acting in an "uppity" manner and considered themselves "above" some of the other members of the church. Paul held up Christ's example as an encouragement to "climb down the ladder" and bridge one's differences with others.

I preached this sermon on Palm Sunday in order to remind the congregation not to get into too much of a hurry to get to Easter. I wanted to stress that Jesus' exaltation came at the price of his humiliation. God Most High became "God Most Low" in order to secure the world's redemption. As such, this text and theme would work equally well during Advent and Christmas, when we call attention to "the Word becoming flesh." In whatever season we call attention to "the humility of God," as the theologian John Macquarrie once said, we must remember that we are the dust of the earth, and that by climbing down the ladder we indeed reflect the mindset of Christ our Lord.[1]

Climbing Down the Ladder

Years ago, I came across some research by Dr. Daniel Levinson, then a psychology professor at Yale University. He had interviewed people all across the country, asking them "what you think about life and how we tackle it." Time and again, he said, people described life as a ladder to be climbed. He got that answer so frequently, he concluded that the ladder is a pervasive metaphor for life in our culture.[2]

Isn't that how we think? Isn't that how most of us approach life? It's all about climbing the ladder and moving from the bottom to the top. It's all about rising as high as our hard work, talent, and good fortune will take us. That's how we think about and chart our career paths, looking for the opportunities that will best enable us to get to the top. That's what we instill in our children, isn't it? Go to a good school, get a good education, find a good career, and go as high as you can. The ladder really is a "pervasive metaphor" for us, and we measure our success by how high we climb. It's all about getting to the top of the ladder.

Paul, however, described the mission and ministry of Jesus in quite opposite terms. You may recall that in this portion of the letter, the apostle sought to address the dissension that was tearing at the fabric of the church. For a multitude of reasons, the united front the church had presented to the world was beginning to crack. The atmosphere was tense, and members were beginning to quarrel with one another. Some of their divisions were hardening. Helping the church find a way to stay together and achieve some reconciliation was high on Paul's agenda. At the outset of this chapter, he reminded them of the things they shared in common and called on them to be of the *same mind* (v. 5).

Now, Paul didn't mean that the church should agree on everything or that the members should surrender their individuality. Instead, he called on them to embrace an outlook and attitude toward each other that would enable them to bridge their differences. And, the outlook he had in mind was the one Jesus himself embodied: *Let the same mind be in you that was in Christ Jesus* (v. 5).

It's all well and good to tell everybody to be like Jesus, but it's quite another thing to figure out what that means![3] So, Paul spelled out what he meant by appealing to a hymn that circulated in the early church.⁴ Let me call your attention to the first portion of our text:

> though he was in the form of God, [he] did not regard equality with God as something to be exploited, but emptied himself, taking the form of a slave, being born in human likeness. And being found in human form, he humbled himself and became obedient to the point of death—even death on a cross. (Philippians 2:6-8)

Linger over those words for a moment. He *did not regard equality with God as something to be exploited* (v. 6). In other words, he didn't take advantage of his position and didn't use it to his benefit. He *emptied himself* (v. 7). Instead of trying to accumulate everything, he gave everything away and poured himself out. He took the form of a slave; that means he identified with the lowest in his culture, with anyone and everyone who had no control over their lives. He humbled himself rather than putting himself forward. He was obedient to the point of death, even death on a cross. In other words, he subjected himself to the powers of this world and surrendered to them. This is what Jesus did, and the text makes it clear that Jesus *chose* this course himself. No one forced him; no one pushed him. The sum total of this description is that Jesus chose to climb *down* the ladder instead of climbing up.

That's hard for us to wrap our minds around, isn't it? We're so accustomed to thinking about climbing up, it's hard to figure out what it means to climb down. But I've seen it, and maybe you have, too. Several summers ago, my family made a trip to the border town of Reynosa, Mexico. We joined Christians from all over the United States and spent a week there, working in some terribly impoverished areas. Our job was to finish some newly constructed houses by pouring concrete roofs. One of the coordinators for our work was a young man from North Carolina. He had just graduated from North Carolina State, and he was an extremely hard worker—a real beast when it came to getting concrete poured! During the course of the week, we had a chance to visit a bit, and I asked him about his life and what he was up to. "How in the world did you get here?" I asked. In response, he said, "Well, my dad just spent forty grand for me to go to college so I could come down here and build houses!" When I asked him what was next, he said, "I leave in two or three weeks for Iraq. I've volunteered to teach school there." Needless to say, I was blown away. Here was young, well-educated, smart, hard-working, and he could have gone anywhere and done pretty much anything. But he sank himself into service: building houses for people who could not afford to pay him, teaching children in a country decimated by war. Not what you and I would call a smart career path! But, to my way of thinking, this young man "got" it. He had the mind of Christ. He had everything and yet chose to climb *down* the ladder instead of climbing *up* the ladder.

That's what Jesus did. Jesus had everything, yet gave it up for our sake. He was at the top of the ladder and, instead of remaining there, he decided to climb down.

Why in the world would he do that? Why in the world would Jesus sacrifice himself in that way? The answer is simple: because that's the kind of savior we need.

In one episode of the iconic TV series *The West Wing*, Leo McGarrity, the chief of staff to the President and a recovering alcoholic, tells the following story to another staffer Josh Lyman, who had recently been wounded during an attempt on the President's life. After some intense therapy, Josh had finally confronted the darker side of what he had experienced. When Josh talked about this therapy with Leo, here's the story Leo told in response:

> This guy's walking down the street when he falls in a hole. The walls are so steep he can't get out. A doctor passes by and the guy shouts up, "Hey you. Can you help me out?" The doctor writes a prescription, throws it down in the hole and moves on. Then a priest comes along and the guy shouts up, "Father, I'm down in this hole. Can you help me out?" The priest writes out a prayer, throws it down in the hole and moves on. Then a friend walks by, "Hey, Joe, it's me. Can you help me out?" And the friend jumps in the hole. Our guy says, "Are you stupid? Now we're both down here." The friend says, "Yeah, but I've been down here before and I know the way out."[5]

That's the kind of savior Jesus Christ was and is. For our sakes, he became poor. For our sakes, he turned loose of everything. For our sakes, he humbled himself. For our sakes, he identified with the weakest and the most powerless. For our sakes, he held nothing back, but poured himself out. For our sakes, he bent low and humbled himself. For our sakes, he submitted to the worst the powers of this world could dish out. For our sakes, he jumped into the hole with us. For our sakes, he climbed down the ladder! He climbed down the ladder and got into the middle of life with us.

Because that's the only way any of us were going to be able to get up and get out of the mess we're in. In this wonderfully concise hymn, Paul recites nothing less than Christ's *magnificent descent* into this world.

Without a doubt we look forward to Easter Sunday when we will again tell the story of Jesus' resurrection and his triumph over sin and death. Without a doubt, we look forward to that day when we can say yet again, "The Lord is risen. The Lord is risen indeed!" Without a doubt, we look forward to remembering that God has exalted Jesus Christ and given him the name *that is above every name,* and that the day will come when every knee will bow *in heaven and on earth and under the earth, and every tongue should confess that Jesus Christ is Lord* (vv. 9-11) But I want to remind you that we can't get there without going first to Good Friday. We can't go there without first going to the cross and seeing again that when Jesus was lifted up, he, in fact, was climbing down, climbing *down* the ladder, to get us.

NOTES

1. See John Macquarrie, *The Humility of God* (Philadelphia: The Westminster Press, 1978).

2. Daniel J. Levinson, "A Concept of Adult Development," *American Psychologist,* 41 (1986), 3-13; *The Seasons of a Man's Life* (New York: Ballantine Books, 1978).

3. Frank Stagg, "The Mind in Christ Jesus: Philippians 1:27-2:18," *Review and Expositor 77* (Summer 1980), 343. Stagg has it exactly right when, also on page 343, he says, "For all its power and beauty, the passage does not make explicit what is meant by 'mind.' The clue is in what Christ *did."*

4. This is the scholarly consensus regarding verses 5-11, although there continues to be much debate as to the structure and arrangement of this text and the extent to whether Paul either adapted or composed the words.

5. "Noël," The West Wing, DVD, directed by Thomas Schlamme (Burbank: Warner Bros, 2000).

9

Working It Out

Philippians 2:12-18

Introduction

Dallas Willard's classic, *The Divine Conspiracy*, deeply impressed me. I thought Willard had it exactly right when he described the popular approach to faith as "barcode" Christianity.[1] "Barcode" Christianity is all about managing sin in order to get to heaven. Once a person accepts Christ, that individual receives a divine barcode that marks them as one of God's own. Getting the barcode takes care of our sin problem and ensures our entrance into heaven.

Although widespread and extremely popular, this approach effectively severs the connection between eternal life and life here and now. How one actually lives here is of little consequence as long as one gets into heaven. Following Jesus in obedience to his way is pushed aside and regarded as optional.

In this section of Philippians, Paul stresses that discipleship is not optional. The followers of Christ in Philippi (and us as well!) have to *work out* what God *works in* you (vv. 12, 13). I see this as a vital and necessary corrective to the notion that all we have to do is "invite Jesus into our hearts." Eternal life is not about the day we die but how we live *today!* Salvation involves how we live now. "Working it out" is our daily effort to allow God to make something of us as we seek to follow his leading.

In preparing this sermon, I sought to flesh out this theme, taking my cues from Paul's words in the text. What does "working it out" actually involve? What does "working it out" mean for the average person in the pew? I stress this because I believe that our churches don't do nearly a good enough job of "making disciples." I also believe that too much of what passes for Christian faith these days is incredibly shallow. Like Paul, I have to continually call my congregation and myself to *work out*—put into practice, live, apply—whatever God has worked into them and me.

Working It Out

During some sabbatical travel several years ago, my family and I had the opportunity to go to Florence, Italy. Without a doubt, one of the highlights of our visit was to see Michelangelo's masterpiece sculpture of David. It is an incredible work of art and truly a sight to behold! While there, however, I also heard another story about Michelangelo. It seems that he was once in a builder's yard, surveying pieces of marble. He came across a lump of marble that was stained, misshapen, unattractive, and cast aside. The great artist took a look at that piece of marble and ordered the builder to take it to his studio. The reason? Michelangelo said, "There is an angel imprisoned in that marble, and I want to set it free."

Michelangelo had seen in the marble what others had missed—potential. He was determined to set the angel free and allow that piece of marble to unlock its potential and fulfill its promise.

That, in sum, is what Paul admonished the Philippians to do when he urged them to *work out your own salvation* (v. 12). He wanted them to apply themselves to the work of being faithful so they could achieve their full potential as disciples.[2] Now, let's be clear. Paul was by no means suggesting that any of us can save ourselves, nor was he implying that we in and of ourselves have the capacity to create eternal life. Instead, in this context, Paul urged the Philippians to follow the example of Christ's obedience so that they might "work outwardly what God had worked inwardly."[3]

In that light, the text underscores the *responsibility each of us bears for our own faith*.

Some years ago, I came across a brief news story about a tragic incident. A family was vacationing in Florida and had had a wonderful day together. After putting the children to bed, the husband and wife, in a playful mood, began to horse around a bit. The wife jumped on her husband's back to ride piggyback. Unfortunately, they lost their balance, and she fell off the balcony of their hotel room and plunged eighteen stories to her death. The lesson? Piggybacking can be dangerous!

That is no less true when it comes to faith. You see, no one can do our believing for us. No one else's experience with God can substitute for our own encounter. That's what Paul sought to drive home to his friends in

Philippi. Once again, as the text makes clear, Paul was thinking out loud about his future, pondering yet again whether he might be set free or remain in prison. Here, he gave voice to doubts that he might not ever be free to return to them. "Whether I am present or absent," he said, "keep working out your salvation." Paul was doing what any good leader would do; he was preparing them for a future without him. In other words, Paul stressed to the congregation that they couldn't depend on him forever to keep their faith strong. They would have to take responsibility for it themselves.

We often forget this imperative, assuming we can depend on someone else's faith. One of the things I take perverse delight in as a minister is taking a seat on an airplane next to a talkative person. Often, folks like that will ramble on and on about their lives, sometimes disclosing things that are often better left unsaid. At some point, that person stops talking and asks, "Now, tell me again—what is it you do?" And when I let on that I'm a minister, it's not at all unusual for a person to blurt out, "My mother went to church!" Or, "My wife is really into a community Bible study." Besides covering their embarrassment, such comments are meant to convey, "Hey, I'm spiritual in an indirect sort of way." The upshot of what they're saying is that the experience of someone else should suffice for them.

In a different light, our faith can wither when we attempt to ride piggyback on an experience we had with God five, ten, or twenty years ago, forgetting that yesterday's faith is never strong enough to meet today's challenges. We have to do what one of the characters in Karl Marlantes's novel, *Matterhorn,* says: "Then the sky turn gray again in the east, and you know what I do? I choose all over to keep believin'."[4] So, Paul calls on his friends (and us!) to take responsibility for our faith—to keep working at it. To choose all over, every day, to keep believing.

Beyond that, however, verse 12 also calls attention to the means by which we work it out: "Keep on obeying just as you always have."

To be honest, the word "obedience" sounds cold and indifferent. When we speak about being obedient to God, we often conjure up the image of a cruel taskmaster whose job is to break our spirits and force us to bow to his will. Let's remember, however, that God is not a cruel overseer. God is loving, self-giving, and sacrifices God's self for our benefit. God, as Jesus showed us, calls us "friends" and invites us to become faithful companions. In that light, obedience is how we show God our love in return. We say "yes" because we love him.

Perhaps the best way to approach the matter of obedience is to remember that faith is a journey. Obedience is how we get from where we are to where we want to be. In addition to all the gee-whiz, high-tech navigation devices pilots nowadays have at their disposal, they first learn to fly and navigate by "dead reckoning." A pilot will draw a line on the chart from the point of departure to the destination. The pilot then will mark out the major checkpoints along that line. Once airborne, a pilot will take into account the winds aloft and groundspeed and fly a compass course to the first checkpoint, then the next, and so on until they reach their destination. The point is this: by this method of navigation, no one flies to their ultimate destination all at once; instead there are lots of intermediate destinations.

Obedience works the same way. For our faith to reach its full potential, we don't have to say "yes" to everything—only to what we need for this portion of our journey. All God asks of each of us is to say "yes" today to forgiving someone, helping someone in need, turning aside from some kind of self-destructive behavior, whatever God might be calling you to.

The good news for us is that as we seek to work it out, God provides the resources we need. Notice how Paul put it: *For it is God who is at work in you, enabling you both to will and to work for his good pleasure* (v. 13). By that, the apostle calls us to remember that whenever we say "yes" to God, we can count on God to give us the necessary tools to make something happen.

Do you remember the story of Jesus feeding the multitudes (Mark 6:30-44)? Jesus had spent a great deal of time in a deserted place teaching a multitude that had sought him out. He taught them for the better part of a day, and eventually the disciples felt that they needed to call "time." They made Jesus aware of the lateness of the hour and the fact that all those people had to go somewhere to get something to eat. And, how did Jesus respond? What did he tell the disciples? *You give them something to eat* (v. 37). So, the disciples hurried to scrounge whatever food the folks there might have brought, and they came up with five loaves of bread and two fish. Jesus took that meager offering, blessed it, broke it, multiplied it, and fed everyone there until they were full. Notice how Jesus used this occasion as a teachable moment. He asked something of the disciples, and once they committed to doing what he asked, he supplied what they needed to get it done.

The same truth shows up in the Tom Hanks movie, *Cast Away*.[5] In the film, Hanks plays an efficiency expert named Chuck Noland who works for FedEx. On an overseas flight, his plane crashes in the ocean, and he's marooned on an island by himself for five years. His only companion is a volleyball he calls "Wilson" (that's the name of the manufacturer). One day, a piece of lightweight metal washes ashore, inspiring him to build a raft and try to sail off the island. He does and is eventually rescued. Reflecting on the time he spent as a cast away, Hanks's character says, "I know what I have to do now. I gotta keep breathing. Because tomorrow the sun will rise. Who knows what the tide will bring?"

I think that sums up our calling. Every day we keep on. Every day the sun will rise. And every time we say "yes" to God…well, who knows what the tide of God's providence will bring? All we know for sure is that it will be enough for us to work out whatever he wants us to do as his people in this world.

So, that's it. Work it out. Keep working on it. Keep at it every day. Because God sees something special in your life and mine, and he wants to set it free.

NOTES

1. Dallas Willard, *The Divine Conspiracy* (San Francisco: HarperSanFrancisco, 1997), 36-37.

2. Frank Stagg, "The Mind in Christ Jesus, Philippians 1:27-2:18," *Review and Expositor 77* (Summer 1980), 346.

3. R. P. Martin, *The Epistle of Paul to the Philippians* (Grand Rapids: Eerdmans, 1959), 111.

4. Karl Marlantes, *Matterhorn* (New York: Atlantic Monthly Press, 2010), 466.

5. *Cast Away*, DVD, directed by Robert Zemeckis (Los Angeles: Twentieth Century Fox, 2000).

10

Between Hope and Necessity

Philippians 2:19–3:1

Introduction

My sermon preparation begins with simply reading the text. I read it slowly, allowing the words and phrases to make their way behind my eyes and down into my spirit. When I can, I read it in the original language, a practice that slows the pace of my reading even more and forces me to focus more intently on the page in front of me. Quite often the words and phrases that possess an inherent tension capture my attention. These snags frequently become the starting point for my sermons. Ideas live in the spaces created by these rough edges, and creativity is often born there.

Such is the case here. In this sermon, I focus on the juxtaposition of Paul's wording in this particular text. On the one hand, Paul has *hope* of sending Timothy to the church in Philippi. On the other hand, Paul faces the *necessity* of sending Epaphroditus back home. Those two words, in close proximity to each other, provided the impetus for this message. Those two words encapsulate the balancing act we attempt nearly every day. We do our best most days to balance the high aspirations of our dreams with the earthier realities of daily life. As it turns out, there are things we really *want* to do, and there are things we *must* do. Everyone's life, it seems to me, has a bit of both.

Thus, the words "hope" and "necessity" became my gateway into the text. These two words became the springboard for my imagination and allowed me to get a feel for the situation Paul described. Paul balanced the reality of being in prison with the hope of sending Timothy to his friends.

He also balanced the well-intentioned efforts of the church to help him with the failure of their plans. Paul's attempt to navigate between these two extremes became the lens through which I read the text and developed the sermon's content.

Between Hope and Necessity

In this portion of his letter, Paul addressed what would happen in the immediate future and also what needed to be done immediately. On the one hand, he informed the Philippians that he would soon send Timothy their way, once his future became clear. As soon as a verdict was rendered and his fate was decided, he would send Timothy to let them know how things stood with him. In the meantime, however, he was sending Epaphroditus back to Philippi immediately. We will explore the reasons for his return in a moment, but suffice it to say that Paul decided this course of action was absolutely necessary. Epaphroditus had to go home, and in all likelihood, he carried this letter with him on his return.

All that being said, what struck me as I read this portion of the letter was the juxtaposition of Paul's words. Listen again: *I* hope...*to send Timothy to you* and *I think it* necessary *to send...Epaphroditus* (vv. 19, 25, emphasis added). Hope and necessity—these are the twin realities that shape this part of the letter. Indeed, these are the realities Paul himself was up against as he pondered his future and that of the church from the confines of a Roman jail.

That's also where we live, isn't it? Between hope and necessity. Paul's own experience speaks to the fact that life doesn't always unfold according to plan for us, either. Our dreams and aspirations all too often collide head-on with hard and unyielding reality, leaving our plans a tangled mess. Life, despite our very best efforts, doesn't work as it should or as we hoped it would. As a result, we spend a lot of our days in between one thing and another, squeezed as Paul was between hope on one side and necessity on the other.

In that light, this text indirectly articulates some helpful wisdom for negotiating the often uncertain path between those two forces.

Accept Our Limitations

The book *Kasztner's Train* by Anna Porter tells the story of an unsung hero of the Holocaust, a man name Rezso Kasztner.[1] Kasztner was a Hungarian

Jew and a leader in the Jewish community in Budapest. When the Nazis began to deport Hungarian Jews to the death camps, Kasztner boldly presented himself to one of the architects of Germany's machinery of death, Adolf Eichmann. He negotiated with him directly for the lives of as many Jews as he could possibly save. He did everything he could. He promised money and goods he didn't have and pleaded endlessly with governments and agencies around the world in order to buy time and forestall the movement of Jews to Auschwitz. Although many later accused him of selling his soul, collaborating with the enemy, and bargaining with the devil himself, Kasztner was directly involved in saving the lives of nearly 1,700 Jews and perhaps indirectly in saving an additional 100,000. Although he was unable to save as many as he wished, he struck a deal to save as many as he could. In other words, he accepted the limitations imposed by his circumstances.

That, too, is what Paul was forced to do. No doubt the apostle would have given anything to return to the church at Philippi himself. He shared such a strong bond and connection with them that it was natural for both him and them to dream of a glad reunion. But Paul was constrained by his chains. For the time being, he wasn't going anywhere. He was stuck in jail with no way out. He had no clear idea when or if he might be released. Meanwhile, the pressures facing the church at Philippi were mounting, and Paul felt he had to do something. So, he accepted his limitations and did what he could. As soon as his verdict was rendered, he planned to send Timothy to report to the church how things were going for him and to serve as his stand-in to help the church work things out.

There's no doubt Timothy was the best candidate for the job. He had been around Paul long enough to learn how Paul thought and how he approached things. He had been around Paul long enough to know what was important to him. Most importantly, Timothy was willing to set aside his own agenda and work for the interests of others. But sending Timothy wasn't Paul's first choice. Nevertheless, Paul accepted the limitations of his circumstances and did what he could, rather than what he wished.

That's crucial for us as we navigate the terrain between hope and necessity. No, life doesn't always go according to plan. Sometimes, like Paul, we're bound and chained to what is, and there's not much else we can do about it. Sometimes, like Paul, we just can't do what we most want to do. We may be forced by necessity and hard reality to lower our sights and accept the limitations life imposes on us. In those situations, it's better for us to acknowledge that and do what we can instead of postponing life by holding out for what we dream.

Acknowledge That Good Ideas Don't Always Work

As we've said before, there was a tremendous bond between this church and the apostle. Their relationship was one of deep and mutual affection. From the very beginning, this church had caught Paul's vision, and they wanted to do all they could to further his mission. Once they learned of Paul's imprisonment, they tried to figure out what they could do to help. (If they were Baptist, they would have formed a committee, a "Ministry to Paul Task Force" and charged them with coming up with a plan.) They came up with a great idea. They would send one of their members to serve as a sort of personal assistant to Paul while he was in jail. This person would not only deliver any money they collected, he would also take care of Paul's personal needs, perhaps buying him food and clothing. Whatever Paul needed done, this person could help. The church adopted this plan and elected Epaphroditus to go as their ambassador.

Now, we have no idea how long Epaphroditus was with Paul, but somewhere along the line his situation began to deteriorate. Epaphroditus became seriously ill, so ill he came close to death, creating a situation that was exactly the opposite of what the church had envisioned. Instead of Epaphroditus helping Paul, Paul had to help Epaphroditus! Not only that, Paul said he was longing to go back. Perhaps his illness made him long for home. (There's nothing worse than being a long way from home and really sick!) Or, it could be he had become aware of the difficulties the church was facing and had come to the conclusion that his place was with them rather than Paul. He was, no doubt, a leader within the church and likely believed he had something to offer them in the face of their sufferings and their efforts to resolve whatever conflicts had arisen among them. For whatever reason, Epaphroditus needed to go back to Philippi, and it became necessary for Paul to send him home.

In that light, Paul wanted to ensure that Epaphroditus received a warm welcome, an honorable reception, and head off any implication that Epaphroditus "just wasn't up to the job." Paul commends him as a *brother and co-worker and fellow soldier, your messenger and minister to my need* (v. 25). Beyond that he holds him up as a role model, telling the congregation that Epaphroditus gambled with his own life in order to fulfill his ministry. He risked everything. Paul employed both tact and honesty here: "I'm glad you sent him, but I'm also glad to send him back!"

This whole turn of events captures one of the things we must acknowledge as we walk the path between hope and necessity: not all our good ideas work! Sometimes the good things we try to do wind up making things worse. The late Maxwell Doty helped many Pacific island nations develop seaweed rich in carrageenan, a thickening agent utilized in everything from toothpaste to ice cream. By helping these nations develop this type of seaweed and farm it on an extensive scale, Doty helped them jump-start their economies and raise their standard of living. But Doty's work is a grand illustration of a good idea gone bad. His work also resulted in the unchecked growth of a particular form of algae that now threatens coral reefs and other sea life.

Sometimes we do the very best we can. Our motives are right and noble. We have a good plan. Nevertheless, things can still fall apart or blow up in our faces. To navigate between hope and necessity, it is imperative that we acknowledge the possibility of failure. To be sure, we distort our faith whenever we insist that, with enough faith, everything will be successful. That's just not true.

Adopt a Particular Outlook

Look again where Paul finds himself. His future is up in the air. He has no idea what will happen to him, and he's concerned about the situation in the Philippian church. He planned to send Timothy because he couldn't be there himself. Also, his friends' well-intentioned plan has backfired. Nothing has gone right. He found himself squarely between hope and necessity, having to do some things he'd rather not do.

Despite all that, take note of Paul's attitude: *Finally, my brothers and sisters, rejoice in the Lord* (3:1).[2] Let me render it a bit differently: "And so, my brothers and sisters, rejoice in the Lord." Did you catch that? Rejoice! Yes, I have to face the limitations of my circumstances. Rejoice! Yes, good plans didn't work out and things have not gone as I had hoped. Rejoice!

Now, let's be clear. Paul is not calling on the Philippians (or us) to muster up some kind of false enthusiasm that shouts, "praise the Lord" at the drop of a hat. Nor is he asking them to adopt a sort of Pollyanna attitude that makes light of hardship and difficulty. No, for Paul, to *rejoice in the Lord* means one thing and one thing only: it is to remember that God is present in all of life. Isn't that what we find in the Gospel of John? Where does Jesus do his first sign? At the wedding feast in Cana of Galilee, Jesus turned water into wine and kept the party going (John 2:1-11). He laughed and danced and shared that joyful moment. And, when his friend Lazarus died, Jesus stood before that sealed tomb and wept (John 11:34-37). He felt the pain of loss. Jesus knew the extremes of life and everything in between.

Let me put it another way. Not long ago, I had sought the help and guidance of a trusted friend and adviser. I was having difficulty putting the pieces of my life together and making sense of what I was experiencing. Despite my prayers, I felt an enormous distance between myself and God. My friend heard me and offered some wise counsel, the best of all being this word: "Remember, the Lord knows where you are." The Lord knows where you are! No matter what our circumstances, no matter whether we are filled with soaring hopes or pressed hard by difficult choices imposed by necessity, get this: the Lord knows where we are. Even if we don't feel like God does, God knows where we are. Our lives—whenever we find ourselves caught and squeezed between necessity and hope—are in the hands of the One who triumphed over the power of sin and death and all the other powers of this world.

NOTES

1. Anna Porter, *Kasztner's Train* (New York: Walker and Company, 2007).

2. Scholars have long called attention to the fact that the word "finally" can also be rendered "farewell," leading some to believe that this notation marks the conclusion of the letter. It is entirely feasible, however, to read this portion not as a conclusion but as a summation. Cf. John B. Polhill, "Twin Obstacles in the Christian Path, Philippians 3," *Review and Expositor 77* (Summer 1980), 359.

11

Thwarting Sabotage

Philippians 3:1-16

Introduction

Most every smartphone and computer has a camera with a wide array of settings. Typically, some features or colors in the image can be enhanced while others are diminished. Certain settings will allow the user to distort the image's proportions, grossly enlarging one aspect or area of the image, and thus diminishing the rest. The effect is not unlike taking a tour through a carnival's hall of mirrors. Although the images are twisted, they are still recognizable.

In the third chapter of Philippians, Paul was forced to counter adversaries bent on distorting the gospel message. Although they retained some of the basic elements, they added others or insisted that one aspect of the gospel message had to be emphasized at the expense of others. Paul saw this for what it was: sabotage! His enemies were working hard to discredit him and undermine his labors.

Although this chapter contains some of the most memorable phrases in the entire letter—*knowing Christ* (v. 8), *I press on* (vv. 12, 14), and *regard everything as loss* (v. 8)—I was more interested in how Paul warned the church and responded to his adversaries. The way Paul articulated himself in his effort to thwart the intended sabotage presents a powerful lesson in leadership, whether one serves in a church or in some other position of responsibility.

For this reason, I approached this portion of chapter three broadly, attempting to provide a high-level description of Paul's strategy instead of digging into the details of each section. While a verse-by-verse exposition would certainly be profitable, I also believe that attention to a broad theme that summarizes the content can be of enormous value both to the preacher and the congregation. After reading through this sermon, I hope you will come to the same conclusion.

Thwarting Sabotage

We usually associate the word "sabotage" with cloak-and-dagger activities of some kind. We imagine undercover agents in dangerous situations, working furtively to damage or destroy some vital component in an enemy's arsenal. We conjure up images of computer hackers sitting in dark rooms, unleashing viruses that will compromise our vast web of electronic connections. Nevertheless, sabotage does not belong exclusively to the arena of warfare or spying. People resort to forms of sabotage on a daily basis. Take, for example, the politician who attaches a "poison pill" amendment to a popular piece of legislation to ensure its defeat. That's sabotage. An unhappy person can act in a passive-aggressive manner to manipulate others. That's sabotage! Church members can work their friends, and others they have influence over, to undermine a pastor's efforts to undertake a new venture. That's sabotage! Sabotage happens all the time and everywhere.

Throughout his ministry, Paul had to counter the moves of those who sought to sabotage his mission. His letters make clear that his adversaries worked hard to undermine his efforts to preach the gospel and start new communities of faith. As soon as Paul departed from a particular area, his opponents moved in and attempted to sabotage his work, either by discrediting Paul himself or by arguing that Paul's message was somehow incomplete. Based on the clues found in Paul's letters, scholars have offered numerous theories as to the identity of Paul's adversaries and the content of their teachings. At the risk of oversimplification, we can sum up their approaches this way: some claimed that the full gospel required adherence to certain Jewish rituals while others claimed that God's grace was so abundant, how one behaved in this life was of little consequence. Some were legalists, pushing rules, while others were excessive spiritualists, stressing secret knowledge and an excess of freedom. Depending on the situation, Paul either had to let the line out or reel things back in.

In Philippi, Paul sought to warn his friends about and head off any attempts at sabotage. He had apparently warned the church about this possibility before and now sought to reinforce the warning. Reminding them of these threats was a *safeguard* (v. 1). In this passage, verses 1-16, Paul sought to rebuff those who wanted to add adherence to the law to the content of the gospel message. The apostle clearly recognized the threat of sabotage and acted decisively to thwart it.

Paul's first move was to speak truthfully. It didn't take him long to get to his point: *Beware of the dogs, beware of the evil workers, beware of those who mutilate the flesh!* (v. 2). Paul's words boil and scald! He identified his enemies and underscored the dangers they posed by using harsh language. Indeed, the tone of this section is so heated and so unlike the rest of the letter that some have speculated that this section is a fragment of an earlier piece of correspondence between Paul and the church. Regardless of whether this section was originally a separate letter or a part of Philippians as we have it today, the abrupt change of tone signals the seriousness with which he considered this threat. Whatever the precise content of this teaching, Paul saw it as a distortion of the gospel.[1]

The key thing to note here is that Paul emptied the threat of sabotage of its danger by speaking the truth. Sabotage flourishes in dark corners and spreads through suggestion. Sabotage dresses up as good and works evil. Sabotage proceeds indirectly by asking a loaded question or by raising suspicion with a wink and a nod. Paul, however, threw the spotlight on the work of his adversaries and their flawed premise. He called them out and gave them no place to hide. He forcefully insisted that faith in Jesus Christ is enough. Circumcision only affects the physical body; it can do nothing to change the heart. Circumcision gives a person a reason to boast in what he has done. True faith, however, rejoices and finds confidence in what God and God alone has done.

Take note that Paul's confrontation of these troublemakers was not confrontation for the sake of confrontation. Indeed, when we review Jesus' ministry, we find that he rarely resorted to direct confrontation.[2] Still, he never shied away from speaking or acting in the truth, as needed. Churches should aim to build people up, not tear them down. Nevertheless, there are moments when there's a lot at stake, and the only way to head off any potential sabotage is to be as forthright as possible.

In his second move, Paul appealed to his experience as a way of negating the claims of the saboteurs. I find it interesting that Paul dealt with the threat posed by this false teaching, not by offering a point-by-point rebuttal of it, but by talking about where he'd been and how Christ had changed his life. This appeal was likely successful because Paul was less interested in winning minds than in winning hearts.

Years ago, I read about what test pilots did when they pushed the boundaries too far in an untried aircraft. If the plane began to twist or spin erratically and go out of control, the test pilot would describe over the radio to ground personnel how the aircraft was behaving. He would stay with the aircraft as long as possible, reciting all the procedures he tried in order to regain control: "I've tried this and this and this. Nothing has worked. I'm about to try this." Relating the details of his experience would provide a helpful guide for future pilots who might find themselves in a similar situation. The test pilot's experience would likely result in some sort of engineering fix or become a part of an emergency-procedures manual.

"I've tried that." That's the essence of Paul's testimony in verses 4-6. He recited his resume as *a Hebrew born of Hebrews* (v. 5). By birth, training, and zeal, he excelled in everything his heritage required. He even went so far as to proclaim that in terms of *righteousness under the law*, he was blameless (v. 6). He had done everything required, and he had done it exceedingly well. He was not a tortured soul seeking relief. He was not a broken man seeking wholeness. He was, however, a person who had been claimed by Jesus Christ and found that God's grace in Christ overshadowed and exceeded everything he had ever known before. By recalling his past and his heritage, Paul was in essence saying, "I've tried that. I've been down that path. I know where it leads. I've found a different path that is worth everything." The new life he had in Christ far surpassed everything he had once known and lived. He willingly resigned it all to the compost pile for what he called *the surpassing value of knowing Christ Jesus my Lord* (v. 8).

By means of this testimony, Paul defined himself in contrast to his adversaries. Thwarting sabotage requires just such a self-defining move on the part of leaders. Allowing others to define us enables sabotage to persist. Defining ourselves and offering clarity about who and what we are stops sabotage altogether.

Finally, Paul countered the potential sabotage by offering an alternative vision.

Whatever the identity of Paul's adversaries and the precise content of their teaching, the one thing they insisted on was that if the Philippians adopted their way, they would be *complete*. They would have the right kind of faith, the right kind of belief, and all would be well. Sabotage flourishes in an environment that is resistant to change. Daily-life saboteurs work hard to maintain things as they are instead of devoting energy to making things better. I imagine if the Philippians adopted the teachings of Paul's opponents, they would soon fall prey to the deadliest enemy in the life of faith: complacency!

One of the hopeful signs I see in congregational life is a growing dissatisfaction with a "checklist" approach to faith. The checklist view of faithfulness requires adherence and assent to an established list of prescribed beliefs. A "yes" answer means one has faith. This approach promotes faithfulness in terms of having the right stance on all the issues. As Paul was aware from his own experience, this approach quickly breeds an attitude of self-righteousness or *confidence in the flesh* (v. 4). Having all the right answers and having submitted to all the rituals doesn't leave much room or interest in growth.

Paul countered his adversaries by putting himself forward as one, who for all his rich experience with the grace of God, was still incomplete and still in process. His personal image of following Christ wasn't a checklist but a marathon:

> Not that I have already obtained this or have already reached the goal; but I press on to make it my own, because Christ Jesus has made me his own. Beloved, I do not consider that I have made it my own; but this one thing I do: forgetting what lies behind and straining forward to what lies ahead, I press on toward the goal for the prize of the heavenly call of God in Christ Jesus. (vv. 12-14)

Do you catch the vibrancy in Paul's confession? "I'm not there yet! I'm restless, and I yearn to be made complete. I'm pressing forward, and I'm leaning into the finish!"

What is your personal image or picture of what it means to be a follower of Jesus Christ? How do we explain why and how we attempt to walk by faith? For Paul, it was the image of a race, a long race. By that image, he sought to convey to the church that despite what his adversaries promised, completion in this life—having it all together—is just not consistent with the gospel.

Whenever and wherever we find our efforts to be faithful undermined, I find Paul's strategy for thwarting sabotage to be an extremely healthy approach. Devotion to truth, defining ourselves by speaking out of our experience, and a fierce determination not to yield to complacency: these things mark the path to a mature and uncompromised faith.

NOTES

1. Fred B. Craddock, *Philippians* (Atlanta: John Knox Press, 1985), 57.

2. Judson Edwards, *The Leadership Labyrinth* (Macon, GA: Smyth & Helwys, 2005), 73.

12

A Threat to Faith: Excessive Spirituality

Philippians 3:17–4:1

Introduction

One of the mantras of our age is "spiritual but not religious." In other words, lots of people claim to have some sort of vague relationship with God and perhaps even engage in some periodic meditation or other spiritual practice. Yet these practices are routinely pursued in isolation, quite apart from any involvement in a faith community. For many, spirituality is simply a path to a calmer and more even approach to life. Spirituality promises and promotes inner peace. As I understand it, the goal is often simply to be more at home in one's skin. Carried to the extreme, however, this approach to life may disconnect itself from any concern for ethics or morality.

Paul faced a version of this approach to life quite frequently, and it shows up in his letters. Gnostics (of which there were many, many flavors) were essentially "excessive spiritualists." The body and indeed anything material was accorded little value. Consequently, these opponents of Paul often went in exactly the opposite direction of the rule-keepers and legalists. They insisted that the body was of no concern, and so what one did in the body was of no consequence. As a result, Christians who veered into this stream often adopted an "anything goes" approach to life. The contemporary expression of this is, "As long as my heart's in the right place, what I do doesn't matter."

Having such a strong Hebrew background, Paul insisted that no one could make such a neat divide between body and soul. The two were a whole, so closely intertwined that it was impossible for what one did "in the flesh" not to have an impact on a person's spirit. Although this particular threat receives less space than his prior argument, Paul took it just as seriously and saw it as yet another potential threat to the gospel.

Again, the challenge for us who preach to congregations weekly is to convey the wholeness of life and faith. We take our cues from Jesus, the Word made flesh, to remind our charges and ourselves that body and soul are bound together (John 1:14). Having one's heart in the right place means that one will also take pains to do the right thing in the midst of the flesh and blood realities each day brings us.

A Threat to Faith: Excessive Spirituality

Several years ago, during the height of the war in Iraq, I listened to a radio interview with Pulitzer-prize winning author Jim Sheeler. Sheeler was talking about his book, *Final Salute*, which takes a look at the way in which our country honors its fallen soldiers. In the book, Sheeler chronicles the experience of the Marine casualty notification officer whose duty it is to inform a family that a loved one has died. Beyond breaking this terrible news, it is this officer's job to do whatever possible to serve the family and shepherd them through this most difficult moment in their lives. In that vein, Sheeler also writes about the detachment of Marines assigned to escort the body home and serve as the honor guard for the funeral. Their number one job is to remain with the body at all times and to never leave it unattended. At least one Marine stands watch over the casket at all times.[1]

As I listened to this interview, I was struck by the lengths to which these Marines go to care for the family and for the body of the fallen. Among other things, they demonstrate that the body is of extreme importance.

In this portion of the letter to the church at Philippi, Paul countered the arguments of false teachers who insisted on exactly the opposite—those who argued that the body was of no significance whatsoever.

At the risk of boring you to tears, I have to provide a bit of a background. You see, the false teachers Paul confronted in this section of the letter were known as Gnostics. Gnostics believed there was a clear line separating the material and the spiritual. In their view, the material world—stuff—was totally and completely evil. It was completely irredeemable. The spirit, however, was all good and most clearly in touch with the divine. As a result, Gnostics believed that human beings were good spirits trapped in evil bodies living in a hostile, material world. Salvation came through knowledge, an understanding of the true nature of reality. Christian

Gnostics (yes, there were such people!) viewed Jesus as a revealer of the truth necessary to overcome this divide between the material and the spiritual. Adherents of Gnosticism believed the body was hopelessly evil and therefore irrelevant to the spirit. Consequently, they insisted it didn't matter what one did in the body. In Christian terms, they believed grace was so powerful one could do whatever one wished or desired; it just didn't matter.

Since this outlook was widespread in the first century, Paul had run into this sort of thinking before in some of his other churches, most notably in the church at Corinth. There the outlook had gained a foothold and had begun to insinuate itself into the life of the church. Many members there developed a sort of hyper-spirituality—so much so that some in the church blessed an incestuous relationship as a sign of spiritual maturity (1 Corinthians 5). The philosophy was easily dressed up in Christian garb, and it infiltrated many young communities of faith. Paul knew firsthand how devastating this outlook could be.

Speaking to the church in Philippi about this philosophy, Paul responded by means of a two-pronged strategy. On the one hand, the apostle wasn't at all reluctant to name this approach for what it was and describe it for his friends. He presented the church a very careful and cutting description. Here are the most striking points of his exposé (v. 19):

- Those who pursue this path won't reach maturity at all; instead, all they will receive is destruction.

- *Their god is the belly.* They are devoted to the satisfaction of their appetites and are slaves of their desires.

- *Their glory is in their shame,* thinking that such things are really signs of spiritual maturity. They easily confuse good with evil.

- They are not spiritual at all; instead they are devoted to earthly pleasures and pursuits.

Leadership invariably involves being able to say, "We should go this way, not that way." In this light, then, Paul's leadership shines brightly. He cared enough about this congregation to warn them of the dangers this approach to life posed, and then offered a clear corrective. Without question, his words possess some heat and urgency. He recognized that this path led to the wrong destination, and more than anything, he wanted his friends to get on the right path! As he saw it, the embrace of this approach to life was truly at cross-purposes with the gospel of Jesus Christ. Paul described those who adhered to this approach as *enemies of the cross*, as those who essentially deny the flesh and blood agony of Jesus' cross (v. 18).

Beyond exposing this way of life, Paul then held up himself as an example to be followed. He wasn't at all reluctant to say to the congregation, "If you're confused about what to believe and how to live, so look to me!" To our ears, that sounds like an ego trip, as though Paul was making more of himself than he should. In that day and time, however, this was the primary means of learning. Students attached themselves to teachers and learned from them by watching and then practicing what they saw. Jesus himself embodied this approach. He called together a small band of students and led them through a process where they both witnessed and were eventually able to do the things Jesus did. Also, Paul's stance underscored the need for positive role models in the face of a hostile culture. Like those early Christians, we sometimes need to see, rather than be told, what we can become. Having someone to look up to and show us how it's done isn't a bad thing at all.

In every way, then, we can see how seriously Paul took this threat, and how he sought to guard his friends in Philippi against its influence. But how do we translate this threat into our own day and time? How does what happened then matter to us today?

One point of intersection is the fact that you and I live in a consumer culture. Unlike the Gnostics of Paul's day, we are tempted to move in the opposite direction. Instead of saying stuff is evil, we have crowned it the ultimate good: the more, the better! Our industrial/technological society has made more material goods available to us on an unprecedented scale. Our mailboxes bulge with catalogs offering tons of stuff and credit cards promising free money with which to buy it all. The message we get every day is that our chief end is to satisfy our desires, to get what we want and what we think we need. Yes, our god is our belly!

Furthermore, I think the text speaks to our confusion about what a spiritual life really is. At times, we are prone to dismiss this world and the things that go with living in it. We have at times an almost otherworldly notion of what a spiritual life looks like and we disconnect it from the rough and tumble of daily living. So, we may say, "I could be more spiritual if I didn't have all this other stuff to do." Certainly, that statement captures the pressures we all face living out our commitment to God in the midst of a thousand competing obligations. But in a way, it is a denial of the way God works. If, for example, you and I pray for patience, how do you suppose God is going to work that into our lives? Not by waving a magic wand over us or sprinkling us with holy water? We won't ask, then BAM!—we're patient. No way! Chances are we're going to run into a lot of difficult people and situations where we will have to work at learning this virtue. You see, it's not about getting *out* of it but getting more into it and recognizing what lurks beneath the surface! It's all about recognizing that the tedium of our days and the ebb and flow of circumstances are the instruments by which God forms us into his people.

In other words, the body matters.

The theological foundation of this way of thinking is nothing less than the resurrection:

> But our citizenship is in heaven, and it is from there that we are expecting a Savior, the Lord Jesus Christ. He will transform the body of our humiliation that it may be conformed to the body of his glory by the power that also enables him to make all things subject to himself. (vv. 20-21)

The central message of the resurrection of Jesus Christ is that the body matters! Paul insisted God will raise *this* body.

Read through the accounts of the resurrection, and without fail, they all emphasize the *bodily* appearance of Jesus. He ate with his friends. He walked with them. He allowed them to touch him. In every way possible, he was with them. Jesus wasn't raised from the dead as a spirit—no! He was raised in a glorified body. And in raising Jesus, God forever said to all of us, "You matter. Your life matters. Your body matters. And what you do *in the body* matters!"

Elsewhere, Paul summed it up for us beautifully: *You have been bought with a price. Therefore, glorify God, not in your spirit but in your body.* (1 Corinthians 6:20, my rendering). We will avoid the dangers of excessive spirituality by embracing the world as we find it day in and day out. Do not retreat from it. We will avoid the trap of divorcing body and soul by seeking to get more *into* life as it is rather than seeking to *get out* of it.

NOTE

1. Terry Gross, interview with Jim Sheeler, *Fresh Air*, NPR, 30 April 2008.

13

Living Up to Our Name

Philippians 4:1-3

Introduction

The names of persons in the New Testament often reveal their character or some quirk of personality. For example, Jesus nicknamed Simon "Peter," or "rock." It's an ironic name because Peter had all the stability of mercury. In the letter to Philemon, Paul plays on the name of the slave, Onesimus, describing how he has moved from uselessness to usefulness through his conversion. Even the name of the person to whom Luke addressed his Gospel and the book of Acts, Theophilus, is suggestive. The name means "lover of God," and raises the possibility that Theophilus could be a particular person or anyone who loves God.

To help the church at Philippi address some of its problems, Paul called on one of the members there to step in. He asked his "loyal companion" to provide help and assistance to specific members (v. 3). The name of this friend is Syzygus, which means "yokefellow." Again, the name describes something essential in his character. He yoked or linked himself to others in an effort to get them to move purposefully in the same direction. Paul essentially asked Syzygus to live up to his name.

Conflict is an inevitable reality in congregational life. Left unresolved, conflict festers, drains energy, and hinders congregations in the pursuit of their mission. Real people have to step up to defuse conflict and get the church moving together rather than apart. In this sermon, I attempted to flesh out the situation Paul referenced in these verses and explain why he chose Syzygus to carry out this vital task. Openly acknowledging conflict, affirming all members despite differences, and having someone who knows the situation firsthand are key elements in a church getting back to the place where they are *of the same mind* (v. 2).

Living Up to Our Name

Several years ago, a friend loaned me a very interesting book entitled, *Letters of the Century*.[1] It's a compendium of some four hundred letters written by famous and ordinary folks during the twentieth century. As such, it illumines the way in which the events of the last hundred years shaped people's lives. I browsed through the book before returning it, and as I did, I realized that many of the letters were intensely personal and private and never intended for public consumption. I had the sense that I really was reading someone else's mail.

When we come to this portion of the letter to the Philippians, I think we might have the same sort of feeling. After all, these verses are intensely personal and specific. Paul takes us into the most private part of his conversation with this church and leaves nothing out. You see, at different places in the letter, Paul has called on the church to put aside their differences and find a way to stay together—but only in the most general terms. We've caught glimpses of the problem—how dissension and discord had infiltrated the congregation. How friction had sidelined harmony. How their rough edges had begun to inflict wounds. Up to now, Paul has presented that in the broadest terms. But at this juncture, Paul gets specific. He is not at all reluctant to bring everything out into the open, and he goes so far as to name names: *I urge Euodia and I urge Syntyche to be of the same mind in the Lord.* (v. 2).

To get a feel for what Paul was up to, all we have to do is imagine a Sunday in which I would call you by name from the pulpit and identify your failings and shortcomings. I don't think you'd want that! Nevertheless, things aren't right in the church, and Paul puts it all on the table. In this regard, Paul's example here reminds us that no congregation can faithfully address its difficulties without confronting the truth of their situation.

To be honest we don't know the exact nature of the problem between these two women. The only clue we have comes from Paul's admonition for them to *be of the same mind in the Lord* (v. 2). Throughout the letter, Paul has sought to make clear what he means by that, first and foremost calling attention to the example of Jesus Christ, who turned loose of his power and privilege and humbled himself for our sakes. That suggests that their difficulties were rooted in their attitude. They were unwilling to humble themselves and unwilling to turn loose of some power and privilege.

Whatever the exact nature of the problem, it was compounded by the fact that Euodia and Syntyche were acknowledged leaders in the congregation. In fact, Paul gave them one of the highest compliments possible: *they have struggled beside me in the work of the gospel* (v. 3). They have been "side-by-side athletes" in advancing God's kingdom. Perhaps that means they opened their homes to the apostle during his ministry there or that their homes were gathering places for the congregation. Perhaps they'd provided financial support and given some of their resources. Perhaps these two women had suffered for the sake of the gospel. Whatever the nature of their struggle, they held an influential place within the church. As a result, whatever difficulties they had were of tremendous consequence. It touched everyone in the congregation. Their high profiles and prominence only exacerbated the church's problems and eroded its oneness.

There's no question the situation was deteriorating, but the big question was how to fix it. How to resolve the difficulties? How to heal the widening fissures?

We might have expected Paul to give Timothy the responsibility of helping the church work out its problems. After all, Timothy would be dispatched to the church once Paul's future was settled. To be sure, the apostle also had great confidence in him. Timothy could be counted on to look out for their best interests and to serve the entire church. Despite this glowing recommendation and his unqualified confidence, Paul didn't give the job to Timothy.

Nor did the apostle himself seek to resolve all the difficulties long-distance. You may have seen stories about some recent advances in medical technology that will allow physicians to perform surgery on a patient via remote control. In other words, the doctor doing the surgery doesn't have to be in the same room or even in the same state as the patient! Paul had no such option. Time and distance were too great. Also, Paul himself had only *heard* about the situation there; he had gotten his facts secondhand. He couldn't be there to see how this situation was playing out on a daily basis. Wisely, Paul realized that he couldn't do a whole lot to resolve the difficulties on his own.

So, Paul turned to a trusted friend there in Philippi to help Euodia and Syntyche sort things out: *Yes, and I ask you also, my loyal companion, help these women* (v. 3). As we have seen so often in this letter, Paul's wording is very suggestive. The word for "help" is best rendered "take hold together with."[2] In other words, this loyal and trusted friend was to take hold of their problems with them—get in the thick of it with them—and thus help them help themselves. Isn't that what we mean when we talk about the work of reconciliation? Someone who is willing to stand with and between two divided parties and help them find a way to come together?

In that vein, Jesus gave us a wonderful picture of what that looks like in the masterful parables of the prodigal son and the elder brother (Luke 15:11-32). In the parable of the prodigal son, you recall, Jesus spoke of a father who gave his youngest son the chance to do life on his own terms. Nevertheless, although this son was far removed from him, the father never forgot him and even waited for him. On the glad day when his son returned home, the father ran to meet him and restored him to his place in the family, celebrating his return with a feast. Meanwhile, the elder brother was dutifully attending to work. When he learned of his brother's return, he was deeply offended and refused to enter the house. His father came out, assured him of his place in the family, and entreated him to come and join the celebration. It seems to me that the father exemplifies what's involved in reconciliation: welcoming a wayward son or daughter home, extending a hand of blessing to one who never left, but all the while stressing that he wants more than anything for both of them to be in his house—together! He stands between the two with arms outstretched, seeking to embrace them both.

Isn't that the heart of the gospel? Jesus, arms outstretched on the cross, showing us how open God is, how much God wishes to gather us to himself and embrace us?

That's what this trusted friend was to do. He knew both Euodia and Syntyche and could see clearly the effects of their disagreement on the church. Paul commissioned this trusted friend to stand in the gap and do whatever possible to find a way to embrace both and close the distance between them.

To my way of thinking, this course of action was Paul's best option in terms of helping the Philippian church. I don't think he had any other choice than to rely on someone he trusted there in Philippi to help these two leaders sort out their differences. I am intrigued, however, by the identity of this peacemaker. You see, it's entirely possible to render the words "loyal companion" as a proper name. In that light, the person Paul called on for help was named Syzygus, which means "yokefellow."[3] As well, he is a "genuine" or "true" yokefellow. In other words, he's done this sort of thing before. He's helped others yoke their lives together so that they pull in the same direction. And Paul wants him to do the same here. The point is, he lives up to his name, and he will continue to do so by helping his sisters in faith find a way to reconcile their differences.

Isn't that how we can live up to our name as Christ's people? It's all about living up to our name and showing that we belong to Christ.

Maybe we will do what Syzygus did. We will join together with people in conflict to help them resolve their differences. We will stand between them, representing each to the other, helping as best we know how to create a way for them to come together, refusing to write anybody off but reaching out with both hands.

Maybe we will attend to someone who, for whatever reason, is having a hard time believing. We don't try to argue with them or provide answers and solutions. We just stay with them, showing them God's presence by our presence. We hang with them in hopes that somehow their faith will be rekindled and renewed.

You can think of other things, I'm sure. But the point is simple: we are at our best when we live up to our name, doing things that are in keeping with Christ's call and claim upon our lives. We are at our best when others look at us and the first thing that comes to their minds is, "That person is indeed a Christian."

NOTES

1. Lisa Grunwald and Stephen J. Adler, eds., *Letters of the Century* (New York: The Dial Press, 1999).

2. Frank Stagg, "Philippians," *The Broadman Bible Commentary*, vol. 11 (Nashville: Broadman Press, 1971), 212.

3. Marvin R. Vincent, *Philippians and Philemon*, ICC (Edinburgh: T & T Clark, 1897), 131, renders it thus, "Synzygus, who are rightly so named."

14

Antidote for Anxiety

Philippians 4:4-7

Introduction

Years ago, I was introduced to the basics of family systems theory. Central to this approach of understanding family and congregational dynamics is the role anxiety plays. Anxiety is free-floating, infectious, and undifferentiated. Put people together, and anxiety will float to the top. Raise the level of anxiety, and it will spread like a virus. People will project their anxiety onto other things. All of us, individually and collectively, carry around some anxiety about what's next. Ramp it up and anxiety can become terribly destructive. Channeled wisely, however, anxiety can be a catalyst for positive change.

We live in an overstimulated, always "on" kind of world. News broadcasts and other information sources peddle fear, creating an atmosphere of perpetual crisis. Fear is the predominant mood of our age. When Paul says in verse 6 to stop being anxious, he has our attention, but it's easier said than done! Nevertheless, Paul's instruction in chapter 4 of Philippians presents some sound wisdom on reducing anxiety's debilitating effects. We have spiritual resources on hand that can lessen anxiety's grip on our lives.

Near the end of this sermon, I clearly acknowledge that there is a huge difference between the general fretfulness most of us experience on a daily basis and the kind of anxiety generated by significant psychological disorders. While I acknowledge that too much preaching these days sounds like talk show psychology, I do believe that Paul's instruction presents concrete practices that have the potential to reduce anxiety's frequently destructive effects.

Antidote for Anxiety

We live in an anxiety-producing and worry-filled society. Stress and tension are epidemic, and the effects are sobering. A few years ago, I participated in a focus group that discussed the availability of health care in our school system. When asked what we thought was the number one health problem students face, I was stunned when one of my colleagues said, "Anxiety." Although his response caught me off guard, the more I thought about it, the more I thought he might be on to something. Students today face unrelenting pressure born of increased global competition. Couple that with broken families and you've got a wonderful recipe for everyday anxiety. Also, a study done at Penn State University many years ago reported that 15 percent of the students there classified themselves as chronic worriers.[1] By their own admission, they expect the worst and continually mull over their problems with no hope of finding an adequate solution. Anxiety disorders are on the rise, as are the prescriptions for medication to treat them. Worry and anxiety reduce workplace effectiveness and productivity, indirectly costing US businesses billions of dollars each year.

Now, let me be clear. I'm not talking about anxiety disorders. I'm not talking about chemical imbalances in the brain that manifest themselves as physical and mental symptoms. I'm talking about daily life anxiety, the molehills-into-mountains problems we've all gotten carried away with from time to time. I'm talking about career worriers. There's nothing wrong with being diagnosed with anxiety; it's smart to improve your lifestyle, diet, and medication as needed to help you grow healthier. But many of us just choose to worry. Maybe we were taught to worry by our parents. Perhaps life's uncertainties prompt us to fixate on all the things that could possibly go wrong instead of trusting. We're stuck on the treadmill of constant fretfulness. And that's the type of anxiety we're talking about today.

All of us worry to some degree, don't we? Some uncertainty captures our imagination and takes our thinking hostage. We can't get a problem or difficulty off our minds. We constantly play "What if?" games in our heads and construct all kinds of scenarios about how things might work out and all the steps we'd need to take in each one. Our minds get in a rut, and we can't stop thinking about whatever it is. As a result, we become agitated, restless, and distracted. In fact, we can get so distracted with what might be, we can't focus on what is. When that happens, we lose whatever sense of peace we might have had. In that light, anxiety results from our efforts to think life rather than live it. Anxiety springs from our habit of carrying the future into the present.

The Philippians also had reasons to be worried and anxious. To be sure, they were anxious about their future and Paul's fate. Facing persecution, they had reasons to worry about what tomorrow might bring. Would they wind up in prison? Would they be on the receiving end of hostility and persecution? And, they were concerned about Paul, their father in faith. Would he live or die? Would they ever see him again? What would happen to *them* if he died? They had lots of reasons to be anxious.

Paul wisely anticipated that his status as a prisoner, whose fate remained undecided, might provoke some additional anxiety on their part. For that reason, he offered these words to the congregation. Now, let us be clear: this portion of Paul's letter was not written as some sort of pop-psychology approach to worry and anxiety. The truth is, anxiety disorders can indeed be crippling and frequently require more than a little self-help advice. Daily fretfulness is not in the same class as clinical depression or debilitating anxiety. Nevertheless, Paul's words here put us in touch with some ancient and essential wisdom that can enable us to quiet the storms of anxiety that so often rage within.

Paul begins by calling on the church to cultivate an attitude of joyful trust. He opens with what many consider to be the hallmark of this letter, a summons to joy: *Rejoice in the Lord always; again I will say, Rejoice.* (v. 4).[2] These words were by no means an empty phrase for the apostle. Paul, we must remember, penned these words from the cramped confines of a Roman jail. He was in chains, bound and deprived of freedom. Yet, in the midst of such circumstances, Paul found that he could indeed rejoice, recognizing that even though he was locked in, God was by no means locked out. As he noted in the opening chapter, Paul discovered that his imprisonment, far from hindering the fulfillment of God's purpose, had actually become the means by which the gospel could be preached more widely. Once again, the apostle found that beneath the circumstances of his daily life ran the strong and steady current of God's purpose. His call to rejoice is not merely to summon up some temporary happiness or fleeting delight but to remember that all of life is in God's hands. This is indeed the source of indestructible joy. We rejoice always, and we rejoice in the Lord because, as the Psalmist puts it, *my times are in your hand* (Psalm 31:15).

Come to think of it, isn't that the source of much of our anxiety and worry—we take too much into our own hands? We decide to take responsibility for the whole world, and as a result, we assume that all of the world's problems and troubles are somehow our fault. Or maybe, we just make our problems bigger than they really are and become experts in turning small things into huge catastrophes. This is the way with daily life's anxieties; we just take too much into our own hands.

Isn't this one way we can begin to defeat the demons of worry and anxiety, by remembering that all of our lives are in God's good and capable hands? When you and I cultivate a spirit of joyful trust in God's goodness, when we believe that life is not an accident but a purposeful venture, then we will have taken a hopeful step in putting our own anxiety and our fear to flight.

Paul also invited them to focus on the presence of God, promising in verse 5, *the Lord is near.*

Over three hundred years ago, a monk named Brother Lawrence came up with what he called "the practice of the presence of God."[3] By that, he meant the discipline of reminding oneself of God's nearness no matter what. He insisted that all of life could be made available to God, no matter whether one was scrambling around in the kitchen or spending time on one's knees before God. God was equally present in both. He continually sought to remind himself that God was near no matter what.

Long before Brother Lawrence incorporated this practice into his life, the psalmist rejoiced in God's inescapable nearness:

> Where can I go from your spirit? Or where can I flee from your presence? If I ascend to heaven, you are there; if I make my bed in Sheol, you are there. If I take the wings of the morning and settle at the farthest limits of the sea, even there your hand shall lead me, and your right hand shall hold me fast. (Psalm 139:7-10)

Indeed, there is no place I can go that God is not there!

Isn't this the indispensable truth of our faith—that God has drawn near to us in the person of Jesus Christ? As John puts it so eloquently in the prologue to his Gospel: "the Word became flesh and lived among us" (John 1:14). By living among us, Jesus showed us that God has drawn near to us in virtually every circumstance of life: poverty, sickness, sorrow, joy, hunger, despair, and even death itself. Is there any place, any human predicament, where God cannot be found? And, the answer is, "None!"

Is this not a powerful antidote to our anxiety, remembering that whatever we face and whatever comes our way, and wherever we find ourselves, God is near? We can put that into practice by saying to ourselves over and over again, "The Lord is *here!*" By reminding ourselves that we are never truly alone and never beyond the Lord's reach, we can put our fears to flight and renew our courage.

Finally, we win over anxiety by handling life—all of it—with prayer. We make all of our lives a matter for prayer: *Do not worry about anything, but in everything by prayer and supplication with thanksgiving let your requests be made known to God* (v. 6). Prayer is an effective antidote to worry. A study published several years ago suggests that religious ritual does indeed reduce anxiety. Students in a Catholic college who prayed the rosary showed a measurable decrease in anxiety.[4] The health community has discovered that prayer can indeed be a valuable asset in the healing process.

Paul beat all those folks to the punch centuries ago. He encouraged the church at Philippi to pray about everything. Notice all the different words he employs: prayer, supplication, and request. Those words encompass all different kinds of prayer, and it's as if Paul was saying, "Don't bottle anything up. However you need to pray, just do it! Lay it out before God." The upshot of his instruction is that everything in our lives is worthy of God's attention. There is nothing too great for God's power and nothing too small for God's attention.[5] That reality accounts for Paul's admonition for us to hem all of our prayers with thanksgiving, to meet life with gratitude. Praying and saying thanks help us affirm our confidence and trust that God really does care.

Jesus certainly embraced this practice. Luke, for example, tells us more about Jesus' practice of prayer than any of the other Gospels. When faced with significant decisions about the course of his ministry, Jesus prayed. When he chose his disciples, he prayed. When he needed to know where to go next, he prayed. When he faced the crushing weight of death in the Garden of Gethsemane, he prayed. Jesus modeled a life of faithful prayer.

So, when life sets your mind spinning, pray. When worry and trouble have taken you hostage, pray. Whatever life brings, pray.

The end result of these steps is an incomprehensible peace. Paul says it will stand guard over our hearts and minds. That's a nice bit of word play, isn't it? Just as Paul was chained to a guard who never left him, so prayer binds us to God's peace. This kind of inner peace cannot be manufactured but instead comes as a gift. It is the kind of peace only God can give, the kind of peace that Paul himself experienced in the dark recesses of a Roman jail when his own future hung in the balance. The kind of peace that puts something solid right in the midst of the swirling currents of our lives and says, "No matter what, everything—*everything*—will be all right."

NOTES

1. Nancy Wartlik, "Win the Worry War!" *McCall's* (February 1996), 103.

2. The word for "rejoice" can also be rendered "farewell."

3. Brother Lawrence, *The Practice of the Presence of God* (Pittsburgh: Whitaker House, 1982).

4. Matthew W. Anastasi and Andrew B. Newberg, "A Preliminary Study of the Acute Effects of Religious Ritual on Anxiety," *The Journal of Alternative and Complementary Medicine 14* (1 March 2008), 163-65.

5. Marvin R. Vincent, *Philippians and Philemon*, ICC (Edinburgh: T & T Clark, 1897), 134.

15

Thinking and Doing

Philippians 4:8-9

Introduction

My earliest understanding of faith was a checklist approach to Christianity. Following Jesus was reduced to *refraining* from certain behaviors. As long as one didn't do the things that were on the list, then one was a "good Christian." Following Jesus was less about what one did and more about what one didn't do. Unfortunately, I found out that this approach to my faith led me to be quite judgmental of those who didn't follow the same rules as I did. Unless they adhered to the same checklist I'd been given then they were outside the faith, and I tended to shun such folks. I discovered early on that what I thought influenced how I acted.

That's a negative example, but I believe the lessons still apply. In this section of the letter to the Philippians, Paul linked the importance of thinking *and* doing. By calling on his brothers and sisters to focus on the things that were good, right, and noble, he nudged them to act in ways that were good, right, and noble. I have known people who have developed a real talent for believing the worst about others or life itself. As a result, they tend to be suspicious, wary, and unable to let go and live. On the other hand, I have met many folks who believed life was good and that people were more alike than different. These persons approached life with a generous spirit and tended to be gracious and forgiving. In both instances, thinking and doing were harnessed together.

In this sermon I focused on the fact that we live so fast these days, and so much seems to work against our being whole that we often lack a solid and stable connection between our thinking and doing. We spend a lot of time reacting or acting on impulse. This portion of Paul's letter asks us to give ourselves to the things that actually reflect what God is like, things that are noble, pure, honest, and commendable. If we seek these things, they will likely become a part of us, and we will begin doing things that are noble, pure, honest, and commendable. And not because such things are on the list, either! We'll do them because that's what we've become!

Thinking and Doing

The New Testament story of Jesus' healing of the Gerasene demoniac is a parable for our time (see Mark 5:1-20; Matthew 8:28-34; Luke 8:26-39). As the Gospels tell it, one day Jesus crossed the Sea of Galilee with his disciples and made landfall on the eastern shore. They had no sooner stepped out of the boat than they were greeted by a deeply suffering human being. Possessed by all manner of evil spirits, this man was horribly broken and undone—so much so he made his home in a nearby cemetery and often inflicted harm on himself by cutting himself with stones. Night and day he howled loudly, sounds that terrified those who lived in the nearby village. To keep him from harming himself, some of those same villagers had tried to restrain him with shackles and chains, but even when they managed to bind him, he was so strong he broke out of them. When he confronted Jesus, he raged at him, revealing very clearly his fragmented spirit. Jesus responded by asking this man his name, and from somewhere deep inside, he offered the telling and troubling answer: "My name is Legion; for we are many" (Mark 5:9). Deep inside this man, a multitude of voices shouted incessantly and vied for control of his life. Could there be any clearer portrait of a disintegrated personality, a person whose life had come absolutely apart? He had no center and was unable to take care of himself. He wasn't at home in his own skin and possessed no trace of inner peace.

I have an idea many of us, hearing that story, might say, "That's me!" That's the way I feel. We may not be all that far removed from his kind of living death. There are too many voices inside and out clamoring for our attention. We are pulled in so many different directions, and we are constantly running here and there. We feel as though we have lost ourselves. We are imprisoned in ourselves, cut off from meaningful, sustaining relationships.

In other words, like the Gerasene demoniac, our lives lack integrity—a sense of wholeness and soundness. We lack the serenity and peace born of the confidence that we are living rightly.[1]

Paul was evidently deeply concerned that the church at Philippi might come unglued as a result of the pressures they faced. In verses 4-7, he stressed that by praying about everything they faced, they would experience God's peace. And here, at the close of these brief verses, the apostle once again extends the promise of God's peace. This repeated emphasis on peace suggests that Paul was very much aware of the forces pulling the church this way and that, and he recognized its potential to disfigure their souls. So, once again, he sought to instruct the church in the right way of living so as to help them recover a sense of wholeness. By listening in on that conversation, we too can find a way to remain whole in a world that threatens to pull us apart.

According to Paul, the first step is to practice a certain habit of thinking. The first step is to cultivate a particular kind of outlook, to think right.

"Perception is reality," so the saying goes. And by and large, it's true. The way we think about something reflects what we believe it to be. Years ago, I clipped a couple of articles that reported that, due to news coverage of violent crime (you know, "If it bleeds, it leads!"), many Americans worried about becoming victims of violent crime. Because the coverage of such events was so prevalent, many came to believe that violent crime was epidemic—even though, when the article was written, violent crime had actually decreased significantly.[2]

Perception is reality. Thinking influences our living. What we pay attention to and give our minds to affects our understanding of reality in a very powerful way. Watch a grisly movie late at night, and when we go to bed, we may try to sleep with our eyes open! We hear every creak in the house, and every unusual noise convinces us that some intruder has broken into our home and is intent on doing us harm. Hear a news report of the crash of an airliner right before we're scheduled to fly out on a trip, and I guarantee we'll get on that plane with an extra dose of apprehension. We'll count the number of rows between our seats and the emergency exit two or three times and be hyper-alert to every sound the aircraft makes. Or, take at face value the untruths and half-truths we circulate about people who are different from us, and we'll act toward them in a certain way. Fill the mind with a lot of junk, and pretty soon our lives will resemble a dump. Turn our minds into an avenue through which fear and the baser things of life parade, and we will create an environment on the inside in which peace cannot survive. It's true, isn't it? How we think and what we think influences our lives in a powerful manner. We tend to become what we give ourselves to. We tend to reflect that which we allow to fill our souls.

All the more reason, then, to follow Paul's instruction here:

> Finally, beloved, whatever is true, whatever is honorable, whatever is just, whatever is pure, whatever is pleasing, whatever is commendable, if there is any excellence and if there is anything worthy of praise, think about [or take account of] these things. (v. 8)

Make a habit of looking for these things. Fix your mind on high ideals and virtues. Constantly take these things into account.

And the truth is, even in this world of ours, we can find examples of things worthy of excellence and things worthy of praise. Our world, as bad as it is, gives evidence at times that it knows what is right and good. Paul insisted that there is good in this world, and wherever it is, it reflects the presence of God. So, search for it. Be on the lookout for it. Focus on it. Celebrate the mechanic who does the job right the first time. Rejoice in the coworker who insists on speaking the truth even when it's costly. Applaud loudly when someone takes big risks to bless someone else. Those are tokens of God's presence in this world, signs that evil has not overcome goodness. Those good things are there—look for them! Look for them, and we will be bringing our lives together.

But beyond thinking, Paul also pointed out that we can experience the peace of God by doing the right thing. He instructed the church to *keep on doing the things* that they had *learned and received and heard and seen* (v. 9). In other words, the apostle called on them to act out their faith.

If there's a danger to which we in the church are susceptible, it is the temptation to reduce our faith to a purely intellectual experience. We assume that, if we have all the right answers neatly compartmentalized in our head, we're done. We can too easily become the Genteel Society for the Study of the Bible, admiring the truths of Scripture and virtues of our faith but never doing anything. Doing church can be reduced to a museum trip where we show up, admire something, and then leave—our only reaction being, "Wasn't that beautiful? Wasn't that inspiring?" Jesus warned that learning had to be coupled with action in the parable of the two foundations. According to Luke, Jesus said,

> Why do you call me "Lord, Lord," and do not do what I tell you? I will show you what someone is like who comes to me, hears my words, and acts on them. That one is like a man building a house, who dug deeply and laid the foundation on rock; when a flood arose, the river burst against that house but could not shake it, because it had been well built.

> But the one who hears and does not act is like man who built a house on the ground without a foundation. When the river burst against it, immediately it fell, and great was the ruin of that house. (Luke 6:46-49)

In that light, it's not enough simply to admire virtue or to sing the praises of Christian ideals. The ongoing task and challenge of every believer is to *live* what we understand of our faith, to translate what we know of it into life. You see, the very heart of the gospel is the fact that God took on human flesh. God recognized the inadequacy of communicating his truth solely through laws and commands. And so, God sent us his son, who lived the truth before us in flesh and blood. This is what the world is interested in! They don't care about our arguments—they want to see someone live the same quality of life and service that Jesus himself embodied. This is what the world needs—not more words but action!

Let me put it another way. Throughout the history of the church we have often spoken of sins in terms of sins of commission and sins of omission. Sins of commission are deliberate acts on our part; we knowingly do what we know to be wrong. We consciously choose to do what we know to be wrong. Sins of omission, however, are passive. We don't do the things we know we ought to do. We don't do what we know to be right. I imagine most of us are guilty of the latter rather than the former. Sometimes we deliberately turn aside from what we know to be right, but for most of us, we simply fail to follow through. We don't put into practice what we already know. And, as a result, we don't experience the peace of God.

Thinking and doing. We can't separate the two. Both are vital to our life and witness. In that light, it's no coincidence that Paul attached the promise of God's peace to these two elements. We will have peace with God when we give attention to the very best wherever we find it. And, we will have peace with God when we make every effort to live what we already know. Thinking and doing—it's the only way we can pull our fragmented lives together and be whole.

NOTES

1. Stephen L. Carter, *Integrity* (New York: Basic Books, 1996), 7.
2. Walter D. Updegrave, "You're Safer Than You Think," *Money* (1 June 1994); "Big Three's Newscasts Discover Crime's Appeal," *The Atlanta Journal Constitution* (13 August 13 1997), A1.

16

Learning the Secret

Philippians 4:10-14

Introduction

As I read this passage, Paul's strained effort to thank the Philippians for a gift that he didn't want or need hooked me. The situation is indeed true-to-life, and I imagine all of us have received gifts we didn't know what to do with. The practice of good manners requires an acknowledgement of the gift and an appropriate expression of gratitude. But how can we be grateful for something we didn't want in the first place? I have embraced this dilemma many times over the years as I've tried to give thanks for ugly ties, meals that included brussel sprouts, and tickets to shows I had absolutely no interest in. Some exercises in gratitude require a great deal of tact.

Paul, while grateful, nevertheless wanted to make clear to the church that he was indeed fine and needed nothing. In his words, he had *learned the secret* of being content (v. 12). The Philippians' gift was a bonus for him, but unnecessary. Paul had made peace with his circumstances and was convinced all would be well no matter what.

I framed this sermon as I did because I think true contentment is hard to find. Wherever we are, we want to be someplace else. Whatever we have, we want more, or at least a newer version. There is always something that spoils the view and makes us wish for more. All the more imperative, then, for us to pay attention to Paul and "learn the secret" of being content with whatever life brings our way.

Learning the Secret

When Ginny and I got married, we received lots of wonderful and useful gifts, all intended to help us launch our life together. Like any newly married couple, we were grateful for those tangible expressions of love and support, and we can readily associate many of the gifts with their givers to this day.

But one gift left us bewildered, and we just didn't know what to do with it. A dear, dear lady gave us a sculpture of a mother and child. Ordinarily, this would have been a beautiful thing, but the mother in the piece had a horribly pained expression on her face. Also, the sculpture itself was finished in some sort of green and orange finish. When we opened the gift (thankfully the giver was not present!), we couldn't help but exclaim, "Oh, my!" We looked at it from every angle. We tried to find something about it that really captivated us. We tried to find something that might spark some genuine appreciation on our part. Try as we might, we couldn't come to any other conclusion than this: the gift was just plain ugly! Naturally, that posed a problem for us: how do we write a thank-you note for something we don't like? How do we express thanks for something that we think is hideous? Something we don't need?

Such was the dilemma Paul faced. The church at Philippi was devoted to Paul, so much so that they sent one of their own to serve as his personal assistant while he was imprisoned. Epaphroditus was there to tend to any needs Paul might have had and to encourage him and his ministry. The church had sent Paul a gift of money, as well. While grateful for the generous spirit that prompted their concern, Paul wanted to let them know that he didn't need the money at all. And so, he too wrestled with saying thanks for something he didn't want. Listen again:

> I rejoice in the Lord greatly that…you have revived your concern for me; indeed, you were concerned for me, but had no opportunity to show it. Not that I am referring to being in need; for I have learned to be content with whatever I have. I know what it is to have little, and I know what it is to have plenty. In any and all circumstances I have learned the secret of being well-fed and of going hungry, of having plenty and of being in need. I can do all things through him who strengthens me. In any case, it was kind of you to share my distress. (vv. 10-14)

In other words, Paul was trying to say as tactfully as he could, "I am grateful for the gift you sent, but the truth is, I really didn't need it!" Paul, imprisoned and uncertain of his future, indicated he had all he needed. "Thanks, but no thanks!" Although he was a prisoner, he was indeed free. He was behind bars, chained and shackled, yet nothing could chain his spirit.

It's rare to meet someone that free, isn't it? Despite the fact that we are among the freest people on earth, able to go where we choose and do what we please, we don't often run into someone who can say in all honesty, "Whether I live or whether I die, whether I succeed or whether I fail, whether I am in riches or in want, I am content."[1] The truth is, despite our freedom, most of us are prisoners of our own discontent.

The links of that chain of discontent are many, and they are strong. Few of us can escape the allure of our consumer culture and its take on reality. We have literally bought into the notion that our worth and our value are determined by what we can buy. We measure our significance by what we have. Yet, prosperity sows seeds of increasing desire. The more we have, the more we want. How many times do we tell ourselves, "I'll be happy when…"? And we usually finish that statement by talking about getting a new car, a hefty increase in salary, or the latest and largest TV. But what happens as soon as we obtain those things? Our happiness doesn't last. We ask, "What's next?" and fix our attention on something else we think will fulfill the promise of happiness. Rarely are we content with what we have; we always seem to want more. It's the rare individual who can say, "I have enough."

Likewise, many of us are so driven that we are rarely content. Scott Walker, a teacher at Mercer University, has written a great deal about the impact of his father's untimely death in his life.[2] The day before his father died, Scott and his dad got into an argument, his father telling him he had a serious attitude problem. It was a heated exchange, and before they could get things sorted out, Scott's father suffered a heart attack. As a result, Scott says he never received his father's blessing and, in fact, felt terribly abandoned. Since then, he says he has been driven to accomplish as much as possible in hopes that someone might give him the blessing his father never could. Driven: something or someone occupies the driver's seat in our lives and pushes us relentlessly, so much so that we are never at rest. Driven is a word that could describe many of us. Something inside, something powerful, is always pushing us, and we can never be at ease.

Add to this the relentless pace of technology. Technology promises solutions for everything. Technology tells us everything can be fixed.

Technology is the answer. But one feature of technology is its continual improvement; no sooner is a product released than it's obsolete. There's a newer, faster, more improved version ready to come on the market. This planned obsolescence and constant upgrading mean that whatever technology we have is quickly out of date. And, pretty soon, we just have to have the latest.

You can see, then, that discontent is built into our way of life. Our bondage to this outlook gets laid bare when it's threatened. When the economy takes a downward turn, we don't have as much to spend, and we imagine that *we* are worth less. When we get stuck at a particular spot, we chafe and brood. We envy the success of others, perhaps turn bitter, and ponder the accidents of fate that allowed others to climb higher. And what happens when we run up against something that just can't be fixed? We rail at life and curse its unfairness and injustice. We demand that someone somewhere do something—even when no one can.

So, maybe we're not as free as we think. In these situations, we discover how bound we really are, how much of life is really out of our hands. What's out there affects what's in here. Outward events determine our outlook. We don't feel at home with the way things are. That's why Paul's words are so striking: "No matter what happens, I am content."

So, how do we cultivate that kind of contentment? What's the secret?

Some would say, as did the Stoics in Paul's day, that the only way to achieve that kind of contentment is to disconnect from life. Withdraw. Stifle all ambition. Beat every ounce of desire into submission. Cut the nerve of existence so that we feel no joy or pain. Dampen the fires of passion so life won't sway us too much. Don't get too close to anyone. Don't take too many risks. Don't invest too heavily in anything. That way, whatever happens, we can say, "Oh, well. Whatever." Nothing will mean anything because we won't have a stake in it. The way to contentment is to pull back from life.

But that wasn't the secret of Paul's contentment. Not at all. You see, Paul was anything but disconnected and disengaged! Read through his letters and you'll glimpse his fire and passion. Things mattered to him. He was fully engaged, and he met life in all its variety head-on. He's experienced the best and the worst life could dish out. He had been up and down the mountain. He wasn't content because he had withdrawn from life.

No, Paul's contentment resulted from his decision to meet life in a particular way. His contentment sprang from a foundational conviction. You see, Paul had made up his mind and so made up his life. He determined to serve Christ. Period. No matter what. No matter if he had received a gift from the church and no matter if he hadn't. No matter if he was in jail and no matter if he was free to go his way. He would serve Christ. Paul was absolutely convinced of the power and the worth of the cause of Christ. As a result, he could say he had already been paid in full no matter what happened. "In all things, I am strong through Christ. I am ready for anything." Knowing Jesus Christ keeps me craving what matters most. Knowing Christ sustains me when I have little. In other words, Paul said, "If I have him, I have all I really need. If I have him, I have everything."

Many of us can testify to the truth of Paul's confession. Many of us have been in some very difficult places, places that pressed us for all we're worth. Circumstances that threatened to get the best of us. And yet, in the face of those things, we have reached down and found strength not of our own making. We have been aware of the sustaining presence of Jesus Christ. And, as a result, we have said, "I don't know where I would be if it hadn't been for Christ. I don't know how I would have made it if God had not been with me."

This is the secret we must learn if we are to be content. If we have him, we have everything. And, if we have him, we are ready for anything.

NOTES

1. William Willimon, "Thanks, But," *Pulpit Digest* (September/October 1988), 11.

2. R. Scott Walker, *The Freedom Factor* (San Francisco: Harper and Row, 1989), 8ff.

Provision for Our Needs

Philippians 4:15-20

Introduction

Some passages of Scripture seem to promise more than can possibly be delivered. Philippians 4:19, in which Paul asserts that *God will fully satisfy every need of yours according to his riches in glory in Christ Jesus*, is a case in point. Every need? Fully satisfied? Life suggests otherwise as many faithful live daily with a boatload of unmet needs.

The apparent contradiction between the promise this Scripture holds out and the all-too-real experience of faithful friends provided the opening for my exploration of this text. For me, this was the most obvious angle from which to work my way through this passage. Getting to the heart of the matter while keeping it tethered to real life was tough going. I will be candid enough to acknowledge that I may not have gotten it right.

I think this is one of the challenges preachers regularly encounter. A wide gap often exists between the promises Scripture makes and the reality of human experience. How do we close the gap without cancelling out the promise and siphoning off the hope proclaimed? How do we close the gap without sounding as though we are completely divorced from the daily lives of our people? How do we close the gap and tell the truth? This is what makes preaching, if done well, both extremely difficult and extremely rewarding.

Provision for Our Needs

So, how's it going? Although the pundits and economists tell us the economy's improving, very few of us actually feel like it is. We're still careful with our spending, and we're still looking for ways to save money. We still hold our breath when we take a look at the checkbook, hoping there'll be enough there to cover our bills. And we pray the car won't break down or that there won't be some sort of emergency that tips our already precarious finances into the danger zone. We worry there won't be enough to go around.

That worry isn't restricted to our finances, either. We often worry there's not enough of us to go around. At work the demands can pile up. When another project lands on our desk, we have to adjust our priorities and rearrange our schedules to manage the load. We anticipate yet another week of working late into the evening. How much more can we take on? The same can be said of the relationships that matter to us. Caring for our children or grandchildren, sustaining a marriage, looking after an elderly parent, and maintaining friendships—all those things stretch us thin as we try to be present with people who matter to us. We wonder if we'll have enough or be enough.

That's the way it goes, isn't it? Too many demands. Too many obligations. Too many surprises. Too many bills. Too many things to do and take care of. Life can be too much, and there's just not enough of us to go around. We don't have enough time, enough energy, enough strength, enough faith, or enough of anything. Despite living in a world of abundance, we have run headlong into scarcity, and as a result, we are anxious and unsettled. Faced with the prospect of not having enough, we fret and worry. The idea of having to face some challenge empty-handed is terrifying. One of the most pressing concerns we face on a daily basis is allocating what we have to meet the demand. We walk on tiptoe to achieve some sort of balance between the "too much" and the "not enough."

As we have journeyed through this magnificent letter, I've called attention to the fact that the church at Philippi faced some sort of persecution. We don't know the nature of their struggle, but it likely involved both physical suffering and economic hardship. The church lived in a hostile environment and remaining faithful wasn't always easy for them.

Despite those threats, the church had found a way to be generous to Paul. They had not only taken his message to heart; they had taken *him* to heart. In turn, they had taken up offerings to finance his ministry in other cities. When they learned of his imprisonment, they once again gave of their resources, sending yet another gift of money and commissioning one of their own, a man named Epaphroditus, to serve as Paul's personal assistant.

These were costly gestures. Given the adversity the church faced, Paul knew that they greatly sacrificed to give to him. He recognized that their generosity no doubt imposed additional hardship on them. As if that weren't humbling enough, Paul had nothing to offer the church in return. There wasn't anything he could send to reciprocate. He was placed in that uncomfortable position of not being able to do anything but receive what he had been given. And so, unable to repay them in any way, the apostle offered these words: *And my God will fully satisfy every need of yours according to his riches in glory in Christ Jesus* (v. 19). Whatever life demanded of them, Paul insisted they would have enough through God's abundant provision. In the struggle to balance too much against not enough, Paul insisted that God is always enough, no matter what.

That's an encouraging word, isn't it? It sounds really good. In fact, it sounds too good to be true, because we all live with unmet needs. To a hungry person struggling to provide, this sounds like hollow sentimentality. To a person who's desperate for a job but can't find one, this sounds like one more empty promise. Our daily battle with one form of scarcity or another forces us to probe Paul's words more deeply to unearth what he's attempting to convey.

Let me begin to frame an answer to that question by first pointing out what it doesn't mean. There is a popular understanding of the Christian faith that has circulated widely and gained quite a number of adherents. For better or for worse, we know it these days as the "prosperity gospel." I have mentioned this to you before, but I feel compelled to do so again because its influence is pervasive. The basic premise behind this take on the good news is that there is a direct cause and effect relationship between our material prosperity and our giving. If we give a tithe or more of our financial resources, God will make us rich. All we have to do is "name it and claim it." Give, and God will not only put money in our checking account, he'll put a new car (a really good one!) in our garage. Give, and we'll get well; we'll be healed of whatever ailments trouble us. Give, and we'll jumpstart our careers and fix our marriages. All we have to do is get the "anointing," and we'll be able to overcome any problems with no trouble whatsoever.

Paul's own experience reveals the lie of this perspective. Paul wasn't a wealthy man. Remember, he worked as a tentmaker to support himself while he sought to fulfill his mission (Acts 18:3). Also, Paul suffered from some sort of chronic physical problem, perhaps with his eyesight (Galatians 6:11; 2 Corinthians 12:7-10). Paul's sacrifices for the sake of the gospel didn't net him a fat bank account or exempt him from trouble. In fact, his pursuit of his mission often compromised his safety and made his life more difficult, not less. In that light, then, this verse is not about faith being the highway to health and wealth.

Beyond that, the text invites us to distinguish between what we *want* and what we *need*. Sure, I want a lot of things, but I don't really need them. My hunch is you're the same. Our closets are full, our basements are full, and we have stuff boxed up in a storage unit somewhere. We may want a lot of stuff, but in fact, we really don't need a whole lot. Do you recall Psalm 37:4? *Take delight in the LORD, and he will give you the desires of your heart.*

Years ago, I heard an old preacher offer his take on that verse of Scripture. He said that if we took delight in God, God could be counted on not to give us everything we wanted, but to "fix our wanting." God could be counted on to help us want and desire the right things! He emphasized that our wants and needs are not synonymous.

So, if Paul wasn't promising the church that God would give them everything they wanted, what was he promising? What, exactly, *did* Paul mean?

Here's the best way I can explain it: Randy Pausch was a Carnegie Mellon professor who had terminal pancreatic cancer. In his best-selling book, *The Last Lecture*, he wrote about one of his students, a young man named Tony Burnett. In 1993, Burnett wanted a spot on one of Pausch's research teams and interviewed for the position. As the interview was drawing to a close, Pausch asked him if there was anything else he needed to know about him. It was then that Burnett told him that he wanted to work on a *Star Wars* film. Well, as things turned out, Burnett fulfilled his dream and wound up working on three installments of the *Star Wars* saga. Pausch took an opportunity for some of his current students to meet Burnett, and Burnett told them: "I wouldn't be here if it wasn't for Randy." Pausch floated when he heard that. He had helped his student fulfill his dream, and for him, that's what it was all about.[1]

Paul expressed the same sentiment here. You see, in response to the church's gift, Paul said, *I have been paid in full and have more than enough* (v. 18). That's a business and accounting term: stamp the receipt "paid."[2] Paul said he'd been paid, not because he had received a gift of money from them—not at all! Instead, he was paid in full because he saw the Philippians' generosity as evidence of God's work in their lives. Their willingness to sacrifice themselves on his behalf—well, he saw that as a sign that they "got" it; they understood what the gospel was all about. Because their faith was growing in this way, Paul felt his life and work weren't at all empty, even though he was in jail. And in that sense, God met Paul's most pressing need by providing a full measure of fulfillment and strength in a very difficult situation.

In that light, Paul promised the church that God could be counted on to do for them exactly what God had done for him—not so much as something in their hands but as something in their hearts. Paul believed that God would pour a sense of meaning and fulfillment into their lives as a result of their risking themselves for the sake of his ministry. They would have the satisfaction of knowing that they were indeed Paul's full partners in the work of the gospel. They would have the sense, as he did, that they had been paid in full, that they really did have all they needed. They would have the fulfillment he himself had known even "in the extremities of life."[3] To know that their lives were not bereft of meaning or significance—surely, that's the one thing that a congregation facing adversity and difficulty would need most. Something to fill them with hope and to affirm that their lives were not in vain. And, when we boil it all down, isn't that the one thing we want most?

NOTES

1. Randy Pausch and Jeffrey Zaslow, *The Last Lecture* (New York: Hyperion, 2008), 120.

2. A. T. Robertson, *Word Pictures in the New Testament*, Vol. 4 (Grand Rapids: Baker Book House, 1931), 462.

3. Frank Stagg, "Philippians," *Broadman Bible Commentary*, Vol. 11 (Nashville: Broadman Press, 1971), 216.

18

Last Words

Philippians 4:21-23

Introduction

The final words of any New Testament epistle are often as overlooked as the opening greeting. We frequently treat these words as nothing more than last-minute housekeeping matters such as passing on greetings and good wishes between friends. As a result, we pass over them quickly, regarding them as throwaway lines that bear little connection to the substance of the letter itself. The letter's about done, so we're done as well.

Nevertheless, I think Paul's last words to the church at Philippi were thoughtfully chosen and intended to be read as a summary exhortation. As the letter indicates, Paul's future was very much uncertain. These might even be his last words to a congregation he loved deeply. They were likely chosen so as to reinforce indirectly everything he had tried to communicate in the letter.

As ministers serving local congregations, our words have a cumulative effect. What we say over time impresses people not only with the gospel message but something of our character. The key question we have to ask ourselves is this: "At the end of the day, have my words served the mission I was called to accomplish in this place?" Our exact last words may not be remembered but the sum total of our words will have a lasting effect to the health or detriment of the congregation. Paul's last words to this great church not only gave him the chance to say goodbye but also one last chance to drive home the gospel that bound him so closely to his beloved friends.

Last Words

Last words have a way of sticking with us, don't they? Everything else a person says will go right out the window, but last things get velcroed to our brains. Sometimes last words are trivial, and they make us laugh. According to one account, as death exerted its final claim on the British writer and poet Oscar Wilde, he looked about his rather shabby apartment bedroom and remarked, "Either that wallpaper goes, or I do."[1] Well, the wallpaper didn't, but Wilde did! Other last words are not so whimsical and they have a profound effect on our lives. Someone might say, "Right before she died, she told me she loved me, and she forgave me. For the first time in years, I am at peace, and I believe she must be, too." Hearing last words like that will make us walk out of the room feeling tons lighter. Students of human interaction note that when someone says they have a few things to talk over with you, we can usually count on the last thing being the most important. The last issue a person raises is frequently the real reason for the conversation in the first place. It's that "one last thing" that matters most. Last words are important, and we usually hold on to them.

We have come to the end of our journey through this magnificent piece of correspondence between the Apostle Paul and the church at Philippi. As we've seen, despite its brevity, this letter carries substantial content, addressing everything from Paul's own situation to the struggles the church faced. There's no mistaking the warmth of the letter, but Paul's intensity also shines throughout. This was not a breezy, trivial note; instead, Paul addressed concerns that went right to the heart of the church's struggle to be faithful. He had a lot to say and he said it all in the space of a few short pages. And now, as he reached the conclusion, Paul wanted to make sure his message stuck, just in case things didn't work out as he planned and the return visit he hoped to make didn't materialize. His last words were extremely important for the Philippians, and I believe they are for us as well.

Paul began his conclusion with an imperative, a command: *Greet every saint in Christ Jesus* (v. 21). To our ears that may sound like nothing more than Paul instructing the person reading the letter to the church to tell everybody "hello" on his behalf. But the form Paul employed here can best be rendered this way: "I want all of you to greet every member of the church."[2] In other words, this was to be a group effort—everyone in the church greeting everyone else. No one is left out. As well, the word for "greeting" also means more than just saying "hello." To greet someone might involve embracing her, kissing him, or extending a hand to her.³ In this light, Paul's command gives us a picture of what he wanted to happen within the church. "I want you to get up and go to one another. I want you to embrace each other. I want you to bless one another. I want you all to do this. I don't want anyone left out."

As we've noted throughout our exploration of this letter, this was a church that, despite all its strengths, had some troubles simmering under the surface. There were disagreements, and the tension had escalated to the point that the church could easily be splintered. The easiest thing in the world would have been for each faction to give up on the rest of the church, for each group to retreat into itself, and to cut itself off from the body. Paul wouldn't have any of that; he called on them to get up and bridge the distance between them, saying, "All of you get up and greet everyone else, remembering you all are in Jesus Christ."

There is a lot of wisdom embodied in that simple command. Few difficulties can be resolved by silence. Few difficulties can be resolved as long as everyone stays in their own corners. Unless someone gets up and makes a move, takes a step in another's direction, we will never understand each other and the distance will never be lessened. Some years ago, I read a wonderful bit of homespun philosophy articulated by the legendary New Mexico saddlemaker, Slim Green. He said he believed it was important to "meet someone halfway and then take one more step."⁴ Surely, that's what Paul had in mind when he urged all the members of the church to "greet one another."

Beyond a powerful command, Paul also offered to the church an incredible word of encouragement: *The friends who are with me greet you. All the saints greet you, especially those of the emperor's household* (vv. 21-22).

In one of the churches I served, a young lady was diagnosed with an eating disorder. Her case was severe, requiring her to move to a residential facility for treatment. She endured a rigorous regimen of therapy, but fortunately it took and the hold the disorder had on her was broken. Upon her return, she asked if she could share her testimony during worship. I consented, and she offered up a powerful word of witness to God's grace. We were all moved by her word, but the most powerful component of her testimony was this: she held up a basket filled to overflowing with all the letters and cards she had received from the members of our church during her stay at the treatment facility. She remarked that all of those cards and letters were a sort of lifeline for her, a timely source of encouragement for her as she embraced the regimen of treatment and therapy. All those cards and letters were a tangible sign that we had not forgotten her. Even though she was absent from us, her church family tried to convey that she was by no means alone.

I have an idea many of you have experienced something similar. To get an email or a phone call from a colleague with whom you have shared the story of some particular trial you were undergoing—to hear from that person and to have them say, "I just wanted to check in and see how you're getting along"—is often just what we needed. "That person took me seriously. That person cares about me. That person hasn't forgotten me, and I'm not alone." Being remembered in such a way often charges us up and gives us the strength we need to keep at it.

Such was the impact of this portion of Paul's last word to the church: *The friends who are with me greet you. All the saints greet you* (vv. 21-22). By offering this word of greeting, Paul reminds the Philippians they had not been forgotten.

As important as that is, there's also a theological component to this last word of encouragement: *All the saints greet you, especially those of the emperor's household* (v. 22). Paul was not referring to the imperial family per se, but instead to the multitude of slaves, freedmen, and civil servants who tended to the daily affairs of the far-flung Roman Empire.[5] Step into the shoes of the members of this persecuted and distressed congregation for a moment and think how this might have sounded. To hear from other believers right in the heart of the empire, believers who worked inside the emperor's very palace, would have reminded the Philippians that there is another power at work. Even in the king's household there are those who confess another, more powerful, king. To hear from the saints in Caesar's household would have reminded the Philippians that for all the powers arrayed against them, there was another, even greater, power at work in their midst.

The last of Paul's last words to this beloved congregation is a benediction: *The grace of the Lord Jesus Christ be with your spirit* (v. 23). Grace is a word that we toss around so frequently and so casually that it has lost its sharp edges. Like a coin handled too often, its distinctive features have almost been worn smooth. But the word is powerful; it's a shorthand description for everything God does in our lives and in this world. God's grace is pardon, God's way of making things right with us even when everything in us is all wrong. God's grace is power, the kind of Holy Spirit power that can help us become the beautiful creatures God intends us to be. It's the kind of power that can fill our days with meaning, purpose, and significance. And God's grace is promise. Grace is the promise that we can live, right now, as though everything will be all right tomorrow. Because it will. Grace is the promise of a future when everyone and everything says we are condemned to our pasts. Grace is God's promise that there's always more going on than we know.

So, Paul's very last word is a prayer for them to experience the presence of the grace of Jesus Christ every single day. In that respect, Paul ends the letter just as he began it. At the outset of the epistle, he wrote, Grace to you and peace from God our Father and the Lord Jesus Christ (1:2).[6] Just as he bid the Philippian church with God's grace at the beginning, so here at the close he prays that God's grace will be with them for whatever is next. Here is a happy marriage between form and function. The shape of the letter itself conveys his larger message: May your life be surrounded with an awareness that God's grace is with you from first to last, from beginning to end. May you have an unwavering confidence that God's grace is always there and never, ever fails.

Paul's last words were ones the church needed to hear. Maybe we need to hear them, too: Stay together; whatever you're up against, you're not alone; above all, remember that you are surrounded and kept by the grace of God.

NOTES

1. J. Clifton Fadiman, ed., *The Little, Brown Book of Anecdotes* (Boston: Little, Brown, and Company, 1985), 585.

2. Such is the force of the word. Some have argued that the plural form ασπάσασθε suggests multiple readers of the letter. I believe the content and context justify the rendering above.

3. Werner Foerster, "ασπαζομα," *The Theological Dictionary of the New Testament*, Vol. 1 (Grand Rapids: Eerdmans, 1964), 496ff.

4. Charles Kuralt, *Charles Kuralt's America* (New York: G. P. Putnam's Sons, 1995), 257.

5. R. P. Martin, *The Epistle of Paul to the Philippians* (Grand Rapids: Eerdmans, 1959), 185; Fred B. Craddock, *Philippians* (Atlanta: John Knox Press, 1985), 81-82.

6. I am indebted to Lewis B. Smedes, *How Can Everything Be All Right When Everything Is All Wrong?* (San Francisco: Harper and Row, 1982), 3ff., for this description.

Part 2

Philemon

by Bill Ireland

The Church in Your House

Philemon 1-2

Introduction

Despite its brevity, Paul's letter to Philemon is densely textured, and the epistle thus presents a host of avenues for exploration and sermonic work. Certainly, the letter offers a glimpse into master-slave relationships at that time and the potential for the Christian faith to alter it. The epistle also brings to the fore some basic concerns of Christian morality such as the importance of forgiveness and the requirement to make restitution. I think the letter shows Paul in his advancing years and his need for help and assistance. The urgency of his appeal for Onesimus to be restored to him suggests that Paul needed companionship as his days unwound.

All of these are invaluable approaches to the letter, but in the sermon that follows I try to imagine what it would have been like for Philemon to receive it. Although tradition relates that Philemon acquiesced to Paul's request, we have no idea how hard or difficult that may have been for him. The opening greeting perhaps gives us an entrée into the situation since this private request is to be shared with the entire church. I think Paul was doing more than simply extending "grace and peace" to the entire church; I think he recognized that this matter between him and Philemon had the potential to affect the life of the entire congregation, no matter what its size.

For that reason, I shaped the sermon in terms of its impact on the entire church and not just Philemon. As a pastor, I have witnessed—more times than I can count—that events are never self-contained. They invariably branch out and touch the lives of others, for good or for ill. I attempted to describe some of the dynamics of the wider audience of this letter, first-century Christians seeking to become a church that was a home for all, instead of merely a church meeting in a house.

The Church in Your House

Two years ago I celebrated my sixtieth birthday. To make my special day even more special, my wife contacted a host of friends and former church members, asking them to send me cards and letters. When the big day arrived, I was absolutely overwhelmed with an outpouring of correspondence and humbled by my wife's incredible effort. Although I enjoyed reading each and every piece, I savored the personal letters most. After all, in this day of instant communication—texts, emails, social media postings—a real letter is a rarity. A hand-written letter requires time and thought, and those things lend a letter its intimate quality.

Paul's letter to Philemon was just such a personal letter. It's the shortest letter in the New Testament, and it deals with a very sensitive matter. As the letter makes clear, Philemon had a slave named Onesimus, who had run away. Not only did Onesimus run away, he also stole something from Philemon. We don't know why, specifically, Onesimus ran or what he stole. Nor do we know where or how Onesimus eventually met up with Paul, but as a result of that encounter Paul persuaded Onesimus to become a follower of Jesus Christ. Onesimus then became a trusted friend and partner in Paul's ministry. Despite that happy turn of events, Paul realized that Onesimus needed to square things with Philemon. Onesimus and Philemon needed to be reconciled, so Paul sent Onesimus back to Philemon with this brief letter.

In the letter, Paul urged Philemon to forgive Onesimus for his crime, to welcome him as a fellow believer, and then to release him back into Paul's service. This was no small thing; Paul was asking a lot! And Paul spared no effort to get what he wanted. Pay attention to some of the language Paul used:

- While I have the authority to command you to do this, I would rather ask you to do it out of love. (vv. 8-9)

- I am now an old man. (v. 9)

- I regard myself as Onesimus's father, and he is my child. (v. 10)

- I preferred to do nothing without your consent. (v. 14)

- God has been at work in this time he has been away from you. (v. 15)

- "Welcome him as you would welcome me." (v. 17)

- If he owes anything, charge it to my account. Let me remind you how much you owe me![1] (vv. 18-19)

Paul didn't hold anything back here, and to my way of thinking, he laid it on thick! He pulled out all the stops and danced very close to the line between earnestness and manipulation. Obviously Paul badly wanted Philemon to welcome and forgive Onesimus, then return him to Paul's side. This was obviously a very serious and a very private matter between Paul and Philemon.

That's why I was struck by part of Paul's opening line in this letter: *To Philemon our dear friend and co-worker, to* Apphia *our sister, to* Archippus *our fellow soldier, and* to the church in your house (vv. 1-2; emphasis mine).

So, here's my question: why did Paul invite others into this affair? Why widen the circle? Why involve Apphia and Archippus? Why involve the entire church? I wish I could tell you I had a definitive answer to those questions, but I don't. Nevertheless, Paul's inclusion of the wider church gives us some insight into the way churches then and now can work, particularly as they sort through matters that are tricky or ticklish. Here's what I mean.

What Happens to One Happens to All

Different kinds of events produce a lot of "collateral damage." Pastoral counselors and chaplains recognize that when a family member is diagnosed with cancer, the cancer is not confined to the individual. The cancer becomes the driver for the entire family. When one person gets it, they all suffer to some degree or another. This is but one illustration of how closely and tightly our lives are intertwined, either in families or in other communities. What happens to one happens to all.

Paul himself appealed to this dynamic in his first letter to the church at Corinth.[2] Seeking to clarify the role of spiritual gifts in that congregation, Paul likened the church to the human body. He insisted that while there are greater and lesser parts (just as there are greater and lesser gifts), all are necessary if the body is going to function properly. All are necessary, and all are important. The parts of the body, Paul argued, are so closely intertwined that what happens to one part affects the whole: "If one member suffers, all suffer together with it; if one member is honored, all rejoice together with it"(1 Corinthians 12:26). What happens to one happens to all.

In that light, Paul likely recognized that the matter between Philemon and Onesimus, while intensely personal, would undoubtedly have an effect on the entire church. How Philemon responded to Paul's request, how he welcomed Onesimus, and whether he would be able to extend forgiveness—all these things would eventually spill over into the life of the church. To envision this, all one has to do is recall a moment when a family within the church underwent a divorce. In the aftermath, there's a tendency for people to side with one or the other. Different stories circulate. Friends part company. This is no small matter! By including others in this letter, Paul was alerting the church that they *all* had some work ahead of them.

Accountability Matters

Besides Philemon, Paul named two others in his opening address: Apphia and Archippus. Scholars have long speculated on the identity of these two and their relationship to Philemon.[3] Was Apphia Philemon's wife? Was Archippus their son? Or, were these simply two stalwart individuals who had emerged as leaders within the church? The simple truth is that we don't know.

Nevertheless, Paul named them for a reason. I would suggest that Paul included these two individuals because he knew they could encourage Philemon in granting Paul's request. They could also hold him accountable in the difficult business of welcoming Onesimus.

We often forget that extending forgiveness is work, hard work. We act as if we merely have to say the words, "I forgive you," and all is well. If, however, the wound one suffered was deep and hurtful, forgiveness takes time and effort. It takes a while for the person who's been wronged to get to the place where he or she can wish the offender well. We have to act it out and practice it, but it's still hard work. Remember, the letter suggests Onesimus stole something from Philemon and then ran away (v. 18). Philemon suffered the loss of something valuable as well as the purchase price of his slave.[4] That was the reality of their relationship. Although slavery is wrong, Philemon had lost a lot according to the norms and culture of his day. And although he was a follower of Christ, I imagine it would require some effort on his part to do as Paul asked.

For that reason, I believe Paul included Apphia and Archippus in his address. Whoever they were and whatever their role, I sense Paul named them so Philemon would have to be accountable to someone for his treatment of Onesimus. They would serve as his friends and mentors in sorting through the necessary soul work Paul's request required.

Churches thrive when they recognize the need for being accountable to each other. In one church I served, a number of men confided to me that they had an addiction to internet pornography. They recognized how wrong the practice was and acknowledged the disastrous effects it was having on their marriages. I approached these men individually and asked if they would be willing to meet with a group of others who shared the same addiction. They were willing, and I convened this group and encouraged them to find ways to hold each other accountable. I encouraged them to help each other in much the same way an AA participant might call on a sponsor for help when tempted to drink.

This is an extreme example, I know, but it surely reminds us that we are to help one another grow. Why not find spiritual friends who can help you walk through some soul struggle, be it temptation, your efforts to pray, or sorting out some sort of call? We are at our best when we take seriously the fact that we are indeed "members of one another" (1 Corinthians 12:27, my translation).

Leadership Matters

Finally, I suggest Paul widened the circle of this letter's recipients to include Apphia and Archippus because they were leaders in the church. As such, they could help set the example for how the church was to receive and treat Onesimus. If they weren't a part of Philemon's family, then they had some built-in distance that would allow them to show others the way even if Philemon struggled to do what Paul asked. They could also show the church how to support Philemon and Onesimus in this entire affair.

Leaders come in all shapes and sizes. Leaders possess a wide array of gifts and skill sets. Some are charismatic and fill up a room. Others are quieter, more thoughtful, and exercise influence behind the scenes. Some can look at a situation and know intuitively how things need to be handled. Others will have to dig deep into circumstances and gather a ton of data before coming to a conclusion. Nevertheless, all leaders have this in common: people look to them to set an example, to embody as best as possible the group's aspirations and hopes.

My father-in-law was a gunnery instructor during World War II. He was given that assignment because he was an excellent teacher. While recounting some of his experiences one day, he said, "There are two ways of teaching. One is to *tell* them. Put a manual in their hands and walk through all the instructions. The best way, however, is to *show* them. You get in with them and do some hands-on work. They tend to remember what you show them a lot longer than what you tell them."

Show them! That's what Paul wanted Apphia and Archippus to do for the congregation. Paul affirmed the leadership role of Apphia and Archippus by naming them in his address. That was his way of saying, "This is your affair, too. I am counting on you to help Philemon and help the church work through this in a constructive manner." Show them!

Interconnection. Accountability. Positive leadership. These are the things that can make this church or any church more than a house. These are things that can make this church or any church a real *home* for person searching for a warm welcome and the assurance of forgiveness.

NOTES

1. I have summarized many of Paul's statements, as found in vv. 8-19.

2. See 1 Corinthians 12.

3. See, for example, the discussion by Todd D. Still, *Philippians & Philemon*, Smyth & Helwys Bible Commentary (Macon, GA: Smyth & Helwys, 2011), 164.

4. This phrasing in no way suggests that any form of slavery or human trafficking is right or justifiable. I call attention to Philemon's investment merely as a fact of the master-slave relationship in that day and time.

2

What Good Can I Do?

Philemon 3–7

Introduction

The earliest version of this sermon was part of a series I did on the prayers Paul offers at the outset of most of his letters. Indeed, the very things Paul prays for, on behalf of the congregations or individuals to whom he writes, often provide significant clues as to the occasion and content of the letters themselves. The letter to Philemon is no exception, as Paul prays that Philemon may indeed perceive the good he can do by receiving Onesimus back into the fold and then releasing him to serve Paul.

What good can I do? The prayer is timely for us. In our search for significance, we want to be able to do something that means our lives matter. In the face of persistent and overwhelming problems of a global nature, we may wonder if any effort we make is of any consequence. Confronting a thorny dilemma at home or at work, we may wonder if we have the capability or the talent to handle it in a positive manner. What good *can* I do?

Paul's correspondence with Philemon suggests at least one answer to that question. As you'll discover, Paul's request of Philemon invites us to think of the good we can do in narrow terms. What opportunity is right in front of us? Who in my line of sight today needs my help? Save one person and free one person, and we may indeed take a small but significant step toward saving the whole world.

What Good Can I Do?

A recent newspaper story reported that experiments with lab mice have enabled researchers to find ways to slow down the aging process. Scientists believe those advances may soon work with humans. As a result, it may be possible for human beings to live 120 years.[1] We may be on the verge of finding the proverbial "fountain of youth."

Think of that: we could live to be 120!

Of course, that means we'd have to rethink a whole lot of things. If we live to 120, when is middle age? When do we retire—how long could we work? What impact would extended longevity have on our health care system? And what would it mean for marriage? Would we have children when we're eighty? What would it be like to have a ninety-fifth anniversary party? Living longer won't solve all our problems but will definitely create some new ones!

You'll be happy to know that this news story also noted that a survey revealed that most folks just don't want to live that long—especially if it means we'd still be stuck with the same old problems. Most of the respondents said the thing that mattered was not the duration of life but the quality of life. It seems we're not as interested in living long as we are in living well. The trick is finding a way to make our lives count. The trick is finding a way to do some good with the time we have.

That's not easy! After all, some of the problems we face today are extremely complex and terribly vexing. Think about our recent military concerns. That is a problem for which there is no good answer and no good solution. No one wants innocents to be killed, but intervening might mean more deaths. Deploying troops would likely increase tensions in that part of the world, resulting in yet more bloodshed. When we look at all the possibilities, we're likely to throw up our hands and say, "What's the use? What good can we do?"

We face other challenges that are equally daunting: world hunger, human trafficking, shrinking water resources. What good can we do?

Even the problems we face near at hand can paralyze us. A family we're close to is disintegrating, and the underlying dynamics are explosive. What good can we do?

We don't have to look too far to see things that make us feel really, really small. We don't have to look too far to see things that make us feel there's nothing we can do. Finding a way to do some good with the days we have is not easy—not by a long shot!

That brings us to Paul's letter to an individual named Philemon, a member of the church at Colossae.

This is a very brief and personal letter. Although Paul did not start the church at Colossae, he apparently knew Philemon, or at least knew of him. Philemon was a man of some means because he owned at least one slave, a man named Onesimus. We don't know the full story, but Onesimus stole something of Philemon's and ran away, hoping to escape and live in freedom and obscurity. Somewhere along the line he met Paul—maybe they were in the same prison! Wherever they met, the apostle befriended him and eventually led him to the Lord. As a result Onesimus became one of Paul's trusted helpers and associates. Still, Paul recognized that Onesimus was a runaway slave; Paul believed the right course of action for Onesimus was to return to his owner, Philemon, and seek to make amends. So, Paul wrote this letter to Philemon urging him to welcome Onesimus, not as a slave but as a brother in Christ. Paul also harbored hopes that Philemon would give Onesimus his freedom, in part so he could return to Paul, who said Onesimus had become like a son to him. This whole letter, then, is all about Paul trying to convince Philemon to do something good.

Paul's opening prayer gets to the heart of the matter: *I pray that the sharing of your faith may become effective when you perceive all the good that we may do for Christ* (v. 6).[2] Let me boil that down. Paul is basically saying, "I pray you can see what an opportunity you have to do something good, and I pray you'll do it. Philemon, I pray you'll see that what I'm asking you to do is a good thing—that it will make a difference. You can do something good here; please do it!"

I cannot think of a timelier or more important prayer for us to make these days: Lord, help me do something good! Let my life count for something. Let me do something that makes a difference. Don't just give me length of days, but let my days count.

We can do some good, and the letter tells us how: by setting someone free.

That's the real subject of the letter. Paul didn't say it in so many words, but he left no doubt as to what he wanted Philemon to do. "I am returning him to you in hopes that you'll return him to me. I need him! He is useful to me! Set him free; turn him loose!" (vv. 12-14).

At the end of Steven Spielberg's film *Schindler's List,* the war is coming to an end, and Oskar Schindler must try to escape the approaching Allied troops.[3] All of the Jewish workers he has shielded from the Nazis, some 1,100 of them, are now free. As Schindler prepares to leave them, they all gather around him and present him with a gift, a gold ring they have made in his honor. On the ring is inscribed a quote from the Talmud: "Whoever saves one life saves the world entire." It's a beautiful gesture of gratitude to one who went to such great lengths to save so many. "Whoever saves one life saves the world entire."

What good can we do? Save one life!

This is the ultimate test of our faithfulness! Who have we helped escape bondage? Who have we set free? When I think of God's judgment, I do not think of having all the secrets of my life revealed on some kind of cosmic movie screen. Nor do I think of God reviewing all my failings one by one. No, I think of God's judgment in terms of the Lord asking me one simple question: who did you bring with you? Who did you help free?

What good can we do? We can set someone free!

I realize full well that, in the grand scheme of things, these may seem to be small and perhaps fruitless gestures. What good is it to forgive when the world faces such vexing problems? What good does it do to set one person free while countless millions remain enslaved in one way or another?

Here's the rest of the story of Philemon and Onesimus. Tradition has it that Onesimus indeed returned to Philemon and that Paul's letter had the intended effect. Philemon welcomed him, forgave him, and then set him free. Onesimus eventually caught up with Paul and, by some accounts, eventually became a bishop in the church. But the most important thing is this: tradition also has it that the reason we have Paul's letters today was that Onesimus collected them and safeguarded them. We have much of our New Testament today because Philemon was humble enough to be the answer to Paul's prayer. He saw what good he could do and then Philemon did it.

Let's not discount the importance of our efforts, however small, to do something good. It's easy for us to think what we do doesn't matter, that whatever gestures for good we make are of little consequence. But this short letter holds out the promise that God doesn't let our efforts to do something good fall to the ground.

So keep the big picture in mind. Small gestures may have enormous impact. What good can we do? If we set one—just one—person free, we will have saved an entire world!

NOTES

1. "Science could add decades to the average human life span," *The Globe and Mail* (13 August 2013).

2. This verse is "notoriously difficult" to translate, as a comparison of multiple versions of Scripture will attest.

3. Thomas Keneally and Steven Zaillian. *Schindler's List*. DVD. Directed by Steven Spielberg. Universal City: Universal Pictures, 1993.

Doing the Hard Thing

Philemon 8–25

Introduction

Nearly every minister I know has had to do something really hard in the course of their ministry. We have all had to do things we never imagined would be a part of ministry when we first embraced our call. Some of us have been on the scenes of gruesome traffic accidents or suicides. Some of us have had to deal with colleagues who engaged in inappropriate behavior. Some of us have had to put ourselves on the line in addressing a "hot button" issue either in our churches or our larger communities. Sooner or later, however, we learn that these kinds of difficulties come with the territory. It's inevitable.

Still, I have an idea most of us would rather endure something hard than to ask somebody else to do something hard. The "pastor" side of us finds delight and joy in encouraging others, helping them through difficulty, and showing up for them when needed. It's a lot tougher and a lot riskier to ask those for whom we are responsible to take up challenges that are consistent with our faith. It's hard to ask someone to face some violent turbulence with you. That's what Paul had to do with both Onesimus and Philemon: he had to ask them both to do something hard. Paul asked Onesimus to return to his master and make restitution. Paul asked Philemon to see Onesimus with new eyes and grant him the gift of forgiveness. Neither person's tasks were easy, but they were both necessary.

As a result, I wrote this sermon as much for myself as for my congregation. I had to remind myself that my vocation imposes an obligation to ask others to do hard things. Yes, it's easier to do those things myself. But if I don't ask others to take on the hard stuff, they will never grow and will never learn the value of actually putting faith into practice.

Doing the Hard Thing

One of the things every pastor has to do at every church is construct a sort of mental file cabinet. As one goes along in ministry at a particular place, he or she learns who can do what and who has the potential to grow and contribute in particular ways. One learns who can be counted on for certain things: who to call when the roof is falling in, who will be generous with funds in an emergency, who can lead a special project, and who can be relied upon for trustworthy and sound advice.

Certainly, one of my joys over the years has been to dig into that mental file cabinet and match people's gifts with opportunities. Few things have given me as much satisfaction as seeing someone fit a situation like a hand in a glove. They did what I asked and they found some joy and delight in the task. They did what I asked, and the church has benefitted from it. In hindsight, I realize I didn't ask them to do something way beyond their capabilities or skill set. What I asked might have been challenging, but it was by no means hard or gut-wrenching.

I have, however, had to ask people to do some very hard things. In one church, I had to ask a well-respected deacon to go with me to confront a church member who was the source of some very damaging rumors about a staff member. I knew going in that no one was going to win. The whole situation would be ugly. But I could not do it alone. I needed him there. When I filled him in on the situation and asked him to help me, he really didn't want to put himself on the line like that, and I couldn't blame him. But he recognized the potential for harm in the whole thing, and for the good of the church, he went. I have reflected on that event a lot over the years, and I realize that I asked him to do a very hard thing.

That's what Paul was asking Onesimus to do: a hard thing. Although Paul did not found the church at Colossae, it's possible that one of his associates, a man named Epaphras, did. However the church came about, a man named Philemon heard the gospel, was converted, and became a member of the church there. We don't know much about Philemon, but he was apparently a man of some means. After all, the church in Colossae met in his house, and Philemon was also wealthy enough to own slaves. Onesimus was one of those slaves.

As best we can tell from the text of this brief letter, Onesimus stole something of Philemon's—probably money—and ran away. To avoid capture and a possible death sentence, Onesimus fled to Rome, hoping to lose himself among the teeming masses of that city. We don't know how Paul and Onesimus met, but they did. Perhaps Onesimus was captured and imprisoned where Paul was. Regardless, Paul introduced Onesimus to Christ. In gratitude, Onesimus devoted himself to the apostle and rendered great service to him. For that reason, Paul plays on Onesimus's name in the letter. Onesimus means "useful" or "profitable." So Paul wrote to Philemon, saying that there was a time when Onesimus was useful or profitable in name only. As a result of his conversion, he had lived into his potential, becoming useful and profitable in character.

Despite his conversion and the help that Onesimus had given to Paul, Paul realized that Onesimus' past could not be forgotten or avoided forever. As a result, he had to ask Onesimus to do a very hard and very risky thing: he had to ask him to return to his former master. He had to ask him to go back and square things, to confront his past and right the wrong. Following Paul's instruction meant that Onesimus risked severe punishment and further enslavement. But Paul knew Onesimus would always be a slave unless he confronted his past.

That's a hard thing. Despite our protests to the contrary, it is very difficult for many of us to come to grips with our actions. Admitting what we have done and taking responsibility for it can be very costly. Like Onesimus, we'd just as soon run away. At the very least, we'll do anything to deflect blame from ourselves. Nevertheless, our faith insists that we are never truly free until we do the hard work of owning up to our actions. I like how one preacher put it:

> Christianity does not invite us to take off the past like a coat and simply toss it aside without a thought. Authentic Christian experience enables us to face up to our past, to make amends for it, and to proceed to live our lives in new directions.[1]

Paul asked Onesimus to do a hard thing, but he also asked Philemon to do a hard thing. Paul asked Philemon to receive Onesimus and forgive his wrongdoing. "Charge what he owes to my account," Paul says. "I know he stole from you, but I have asked him to return and take responsibility" (vv. 18-19).

Put yourself in Philemon's shoes for a moment. That would be hard to do, wouldn't it? Whenever someone steals from us—maybe not our goods or our treasures but our faith and trust—it's hard to get over it. The residue of the breach of trust can't be scrubbed away. It's always there. It's a silent but formidable obstacle, and it's difficult to put aside. But Paul asked Philemon to do exactly that. He asked Philemon to forgive Onesimus.

Yet the even more difficult thing Paul asked of Philemon was to see Onesimus with new eyes. *Welcome him,* Paul says, *as you would welcome me* (v. 17). Welcome him not as a slave, but as a brother. To do that Philemon would have to go against the very grain of the society in which he lived. He would have to go against everything he had ever learned.

Do you remember the classic movie *Driving Miss Daisy*?[2] If you do, you'll recall that the film relates the story of an elderly Jewish lady named Daisy and her African-American chauffeur, a man named Hoke. As the film opens, Miss Daisy resists having Hoke become her driver. She doesn't want a driver; she believes she can still drive well. After she reluctantly accepts his role, all the old prejudices came into play; she assumes Hoke will steal from her, for example, because he is black. But, as the film so beautifully depicts, over time, Miss Daisy and Hoke become friends. The barriers go down, and their lives become knit together—so much so that, as they near the end of their days, Miss Daisy says, "Hoke, you're my best friend." She did the hard thing. She learned to see Hoke with new eyes. She learned to see beyond her prejudices and to see him. She learned to see him as a friend, not just an employee. Paul gave Philemon the opportunity to do the same. Paul invited Philemon to do a hard thing, something that could strengthen his faith and enhance his witness.[3]

Apparently Philemon was up to the challenge. There is a tradition that Philemon not only welcomed Onesimus but set him free to return to Paul. And the tradition is that he became one of Paul's most trusted associates. Fifty years later, the bishop of Antioch wrote a letter to the bishop of Ephesus, addressed to none other than Onesimus. Beyond that, there is a strong tradition crediting Onesimus with collecting and preserving Paul's letters. If that's true, we are tremendously in Philemon's debt. He did the hard thing and wound up blessing the whole world, becoming more useful than he ever could have imagined.

From time to time, our faith asks us to do difficult things. Following Jesus requires that we confront our past and take responsibility, even when it might cost us. Following Jesus requires that we do our part to make amends when we've wronged someone. Following Jesus requires that we pay the price of offering forgiveness and change our way of looking at someone else. Jesus put it this way: "Whoever does not carry the cross and follow me cannot be my disciple" (Luke 14:27). The simple truth is this: doing the hard thing is the way we all become useful in God's kingdom.

NOTES

1. John Claypool, "Good Luck, Bad Luck," *The Library of Distinctive Sermons*, vol. 1, ed. Gary W. Klingsporn (Sisters, OR: Questar Publishers, 1996), 35.

2. Alfred Uhry, *Driving Miss Daisy*, DVD, directed by Bruce Beresford (Burbank: Warner Bros, 1989).

3. Hoke also did a hard thing to work for Miss Daisy and to accept, help, forgive, and become friends with her. Miss Daisy's hard thing is not more significant than Hoke's, nor is Philemon's more significant than Onesimus's.

Part 3

Colossians

by Dock Hollingsworth

Getting Word to the Saints and the Faithful

Colossians 1:1-10

Two years ago, I preached a series of sermons from Genesis. Last year, I preached a series from Exodus, and I left you with the promise that I would not preach a series, this year, from Leviticus. I am, however, preaching through another book of the Bible. It was not my plan, but this year I got an invitation to write a book of sermons for a commentary series by Smyth & Helwys Publishing. The series will include a book of sermons on each book of the New Testament with no verses left out. Here's the good news: if I had been assigned Genesis, I would still be preaching from Genesis next Advent. As it is, I am preaching for nine weeks from a book with only four chapters. Let me say this in the positive—in nine weeks, you will be the most informed person at the water cooler on the book of Colossians. This often-ignored book is rich for preaching, and I'm excited about the timing for us. It is written to a church like ours in some ways. They are enthusiastic about being the church, but for them, many important things were missing.

Have you been around people who are new at something—they're enthusiastic, their hearts are in it—and yet there are some important playing pieces still missing? I played golf recently with one of these people. He had taken up the game in the last two years. He had taken lessons and had all of the right gear. He had a fortune in golf clubs, all matched and shiny. He is "well to do," so he had already played many of the great courses. The day we played, he was wearing a sweater vest from Kiawah Island, a hat from The Breakers in Palm Beach, and his golf towel was from Pinehurst. He loved the game—you could tell—but nobody had told him yet that he was not supposed to talk when somebody else was hitting. Nobody had told him about replacing divots and repairing ball marks. Nobody had told him not to walk around while I'm putting. He walked around while I was putting! (Okay, I'm over it.)

I am sympathetic. When Haley was little and started playing soccer, I was enthusiastic. It was great exercise, and I was happy to see her in a sport she enjoyed. I became an enthusiast, except that I knew nothing about soccer. I got the simple stuff—pass it to your player, advance the ball, kick it past the girl in front of the net who is wearing mittens that match her hair bow. I googled "Soccer for stupid dads" or some site like that, but I still don't know what "off sides" means.

The occasion of this letter to the church in Colossae is that the good-hearted, sincere, enthusiastic new Christians are just not "getting it" on some really important aspects of the faith. They are new and eager, and in the first movements of the Christian church, it is hard to know which teachings are orthodox and which ones are off base. They didn't have the benefit of centuries of the church's teaching or commentaries by scholars. The Christian church was still in its infancy and learning. This enthusiastic group was doing so much right and yet beginning down a path of danger. So they received this letter to help them realign.

For ease of preaching and hearing, let's suppose Paul wrote the letter. I need to tell you, though, that there is considerable scholarship that suggests otherwise. The language, phrasing, and images are different enough from his other letters for many scholars to conclude that it was written by someone else and ascribed to Paul, which was not an uncommon practice in that day. Defenders, on the other hand, say that Paul has just grown. Paul is not static. "This church is unique, Paul is growing—you shouldn't expect it to sound just like the other letters. Different church, different Paul." In any case, you should know that there is reasonable scholarly debate, but it will make for awkward preaching if I continue to reference the author as, "Paul or some disciple within his apostolic tradition who has ascribed Pauline authorship to the Epistle." Let's just go with "Paul." You know the debate, but it will be easier to listen to.

So Paul writes to the church at Colossae and affirms that this new church start is doing so much right. This enthusiastic group of believers is sincerely trying to be faithful.

> To the saints and faithful brothers and sisters in Christ at Colossae:
> Grace to you and peace from God our Father. In our prayers for you
> we always thank God, the Father of our Lord Jesus Christ, for we have

heard of your faith in Christ Jesus and of the love that you have for all the saints, because of the hope laid up for you in heaven. (vv. 2-5)

"Faith, hope, and love" is a great beginning. Paul affirms their faith in Christ, their love for the saints, and the hope in heaven, all of which are so much on target. Faith, rooted in the past (the life, death, and resurrection). Love, the current form in which faith is manifest. And hope, the future dimension of the Christian experience.[1]

They have gotten so much right, yet Paul is setting up his corrective challenge. In these first ten verses, Paul has mentioned Christ five times. The centrality of Jesus is part of what Paul needs to correct. And why? Here may be the thesis sentence of the letter:

> ...that you may be filled with the knowledge of God's will in all spiritual wisdom and understanding, so that you may lead lives worthy of the Lord, fully pleasing to him, as you bear fruit in every good work and as you grow in the knowledge of God. (vv. 9-10)

And this is why it matters to us. Colossians matters to us only if we are interested in:

- being filled with knowledge of God's will,

- leading a worthy life that pleases God,

- doing work that matters, and

- growing in the knowledge of God.

For Paul to explore these important themes, he needs us first to get right about who Jesus is. Our theology, our doctrine matters.

The modern church, at least our little corner of it, does not talk much about doctrine and theology anymore. When I was a young minister, right doctrine was everything. We regularly quizzed each other in seminary about what we believed: "Do you believe in premillennialism, postmillennialism, or amillennialism and why?" "Do you believe that the tribal Brazilian who has never heard of Jesus will go to hell because he did not believe in Jesus?" "Do you believe with Augustine that we are born in sin and that our primary nature is sinfulness, or do you believe with Pelagius, that we are born bearing the image of God and that our primary nature is goodness?"

We hounded each other. Doctrine mattered.

In the early days of my ministry, the annual meeting of the Georgia Baptist Convention even included a Doctrinal Sermon because right doctrine is so important.

"What do you believe?" was the question of my early ministry.

Now, it rarely comes up. Oh, we talk some about what we believe about some social issues, but we do not usually use words as strong as "believe." We say, "What is your current position on so and so?" We seldom ask each other what we believe.

I'm guilty. I have put more weight on behavior than belief. In theological terms, I am more interested in orthopraxy (right practice) than orthodoxy (right belief). The reason, I suppose, is that I just got so fed up with the ministers I knew early in my ministry who were always right and seldom kind. I was around ministers who spit out their insistence that I believe right, which meant believing like them, and some of them were just mean. I probably overreacted and overcorrected. I have always had more space for people who were humble and kind and wrong than for red-faced people who were right.

But what Paul cares about in this letter to the church at Colossae are things I care about too. I am interested in being filled with knowledge of God's will, leading a worthy life that pleases God, doing work that matters, and growing in the knowledge of God.

And for Paul, this starts with a right theology of Christ. Jesus, rightly understood, is at the center of how we build our life. Work matters. Leading a worthy life matters. (We will get to this in coming weeks, but our first task is not orthopraxy but orthodoxy.) What we believe about Jesus matters.

This eager group of Christians at the new church in Colossae is getting so much right, but they are at risk of building their church on a bad foundation. Paul can't let that happen, so he intervenes. You could say that he intrudes. Paul has never been to this church, after all. This is not one of his church plants. This is not like Corinth, where Paul loved the people, preached the gospel, and started the church. This church might have been started by Epaphras, who is mentioned in these opening verses, but there is no indication that Paul has ever visited this church or met any of its members. If it's not one of his church plants, and he does not know these people anyway, why is he intruding?

Because it *is* his church and because it matters so deeply. By "it is his church," I mean that the Church is interconnected and accountable. He begins the letter by saying, *to the saints and faithful brothers and sisters* (v. 2).

These are his kinfolk. This is his church and our church. It doesn't matter that he has never been there. We are the Church—all believers. Paul corrects us too—even though he has never been to our congregation.

We are all connected, but it begins in Christ. It begins at this Communion table. Because they ate the bread and drank from the cup, we are connected to:

- The church at Colossae, even though it was born about two thousand years ago;

- The new church start in a storefront with an electric guitar, ten parishioners, and an ex-addict for a pastor;

- The church in Santiago, Chile, who will come to the table today and say the words of institution in Spanish, *"Esto es mi cuerpo, tomar, comer"*;

- The South Georgia pastor who preached the Doctrinal Sermon all those years ago and whose doctrines make me shudder. He is still my brother; he is one of the saints and the faithful.

We are all teaching, correcting, defending, and hoping to understand more fully what it means to *be filled with the knowledge of God's will in all spiritual wisdom and understanding, so that you may lead lives worthy of the Lord, fully pleasing to him, as you bear fruit in every good work and as you grow in the knowledge of God* (vv. 9-10).

The saints and the faithful of every generation and every culture are made one and made low at the table of Christ. We are tied to one another through Jesus and through this table.

We will take a nine-week journey into how to lead a worthy life that bears fruit. But the journey starts at the table. It starts with a right understanding of Jesus and his forgiveness. The Jesus-shaped community goes back to when the Lamb of God sat at the table with twelve men,

> He said to them, "I have earnestly desired to eat this Passover with you before I suffer; for I tell you, I will not eat it until it is fulfilled in the kingdom of God." Then he took a cup, and after giving thanks he said, "Take this and divide it among yourselves; for I tell you that from now on I will not drink of the fruit of the vine until the kingdom of God comes." Then he took a loaf of bread, and when he had given thanks, he broke it and gave it to them, saying, "This is my body, which is given

for you. Do this in remembrance of me." And he did the same with the cup after supper, saying, "This cup that is poured out for you is the new covenant in my blood." (Luke 22:15-20)

NOTE

1. Eduard Schweizer, *The Letter to the Colossians* (Minneapolis: Augsburg Publishing House, 1976), 33-34.

2

Getting Out of the Darkness

Colossians 1:11-14

It is late Sunday afternoon in an insignificant first-century town in what is now Turkey. Today is the Christian Sabbath—the Lord's Day—and this father of two is headed to another man's home for his weekly church meeting. Several hours ago, he and the family had some barley, gruel, and pasta together—he is hungry again, but soon he will share a table with other believers.

When he arrives, there is some energy in the room. A letter has arrived with the Apostle Paul's name on it. At the center of tonight's gathering will be the reading of this letter. The place is electric with excitement. Who knows how long it took this letter to arrive? The postal service is for official dispatches only. Private letters have to be carried by a trusted friend, in this case a Christian headed toward Colossae.[1]

The place is buzzing, but it's hard for our hungry believer to join in the energy of the evening. He is preoccupied with his own stuff. First, he's tired of the conflict in his little church. They love each other. They started in such energy and hope, and now there is a doctrinal controversy that may prove too big to overcome. He's tired of the fussing. Not to mention that he has brought other concerns to today's church meeting, for his family and for some of his other relationships. Truthfully, he wonders about his own faith in this new religion and thinks to himself, "What is the nature of prayer and real faith? What endures? What is important? What will last beyond my few years?" He's tired. He's lost patience, power, and endurance, but he's here at church—eating and laughing and acting like he's into it.

After the meal, Epaphras stands to read the letter. The tired husband and father combs back his long, black hair with his fingers and settles in to see if there is anything worth listening to. The letter is from the great Apostle Paul but "The Great Apostle Paul" has never met him or his family, and Paul has never even been to their church. The man crosses his arms and listens anyway: "To the saints and faithful brothers and sisters in Christ at Colossae: Grace to you and peace" (1:2).

After the introduction, Paul offers this prayer to the church and to the tired man who just combed back his hair and wonders if anything lasts:

> May you be made strong with all the strength that comes from his glorious power, and may you be prepared to endure everything with patience, while joyfully giving thanks to the Father, who has enabled you to share in the inheritance of the saints in the light. (vv. 11-12)

The man with the black hair sits up. "A prayer for strength and endurance and patience with joy? Maybe this guy Paul does understand me." He so desperately needs something to believe in again.

My friend Tim Owings was the long-time pastor of First Baptist Church, Augusta, Georgia. Years ago, he became friends with Dr. William Augustus Jones Jr., the esteemed pastor of Bethany Baptist Church in Brooklyn. Dr. Owings and Dr. Jones, this great African-American pastor, became close friends and even preached in each other's pulpits. One day of honest conversation led Tim Owings to ask, "What do you pray for most often?" Dr. Jones said, "I pray my mind doesn't die before my body, that I don't outlive my mourners, and that I don't drown in shallow water."[2]

That phrase, "drown in shallow water," stayed with Tim Owings. Later, he wrote a book on Colossians, a really fine book that has been helpful to me in this preaching series. He titled it *Drowning in Shallow Water*.

Maybe the husband and father with the long hair, sitting at church in Colossae, has this same fear. He has just perked up and decided to listen closely to the rest of the letter because he knows that he is at risk of drowning in shallow water, and he needs someone to speak to his pain.

Today, we are two thousand years and over five thousand miles removed from the day that man heard this letter. We are safe and dry, well groomed, well fed, and educated. We have iPads, mortgages, and luxury automobiles, yet we sit with the same basic questions, wants, and insecurities. Shallow water may get us too. We know that, between soccer and play dates and low quarterly earnings and private SAT tutors and private swim lessons and year-end losses and "will she get into private school?" and one more credit card and another argument with my daughter and the spring ALTA league, we could drown in shallow water.

Some are more terrified than that. Some people feel more like an eight-year-old child than we want to admit. During WWII, the great London pastor Leslie Weatherhead was out one night during the London Blitz, right after the "all clear" sounded, and he found an eight-year-old boy sobbing. He asked the boy, "Where is your father?"

He said, "He went overseas in the Army and he was killed."

"Well, where then is your mother?"

"She has been killed, too, in the air-raid last night."

"But what about the rest of your family—brothers, sisters, aunts, uncles?"

The boy said, "I don't know where they are. They may have been killed too."

Weatherhead looked down at the boy and said, "Tell me, son, who are you?"

The boy answered, "Mister, I ain't nobody's nothing."[3]

This is not sensationalism. I talk with some of you who feel like you are "nobody's nothing." Others in the room feel like we might drown in shallow water. Isn't there some answer to the gnawing sense that something is incomplete? Wasn't the German car, new shoes, and new job title supposed to make the pain go away?

The worried man with the long hair in the first-century house church continues to listen to the reading of the letter:

> the Father, who has enabled you to share in the inheritance of the
> saints in the light. He has rescued us from the power of darkness and
> transferred us into the kingdom of his beloved Son, in whom we have
> redemption, the forgiveness of sins. (vv. 12-14)

The man with the swooping hair, the little boy in London, the Brooklyn pastor who's afraid of drowning in shallow water, all of us who are honest want to be transferred. We want to be transferred to a Kingdom where there is redemption and forgiveness. We want a transfer from the dominion of darkness into the glorious light, as the letter says. We want answers. We want the gnawing sense of incompleteness to go away. We want lives of meaning and purpose. We want to live for things that last longer than tennis rankings and Little League baseball standings and quarterly earnings.

We want to be delivered before we drown in shallow water. If only we were qualified.

How would we qualify for a new life, to be transferred from the dominion of darkness into the Kingdom of glorious light?

It feels good to be qualified. My first qualification, I suppose, was when I passed my test to be a lifeguard. I spent my high school summers at the Doraville City Pool. I started as a lowly basket worker, but then I studied and tested and became qualified. I passed the written test, swam the laps, and treaded water for however many minutes was required. The final test was when Mark Roach, 210 pounds of Mark Roach, blew air out and sank to the bottom of the deep end. I had to dive in and get him. I swam him over to the side while keeping his mouth and nose out of the water. I overlapped his hands on the side of the pool and placed one of my hands on top to hold his while I pulled myself out of the water, then pulled him up on deck to begin CPR.

I passed. I earned it. I was now a qualified lifeguard.

All of that work learning to save lives, and I mostly spent my summers blowing my whistle and telling the Newman boys to stop running. But it feels good to be qualified.

How do we earn passage to a life of significance? What would qualify us to be transferred from darkness into light?

At the center of the gospel and this letter is the grace-filled truth that we don't earn it: *giving thanks to the Father, who has qualified us to share in the inheritance of the saints* (v. 12, ESV). That is the good news for the desperate man with the long hair: he is already qualified. It's your good news too. God has already qualified you to share in the inheritance. You may transfer from darkness into light whenever you wish. In Christ Jesus, there is redemption and the forgiveness of sins. It starts with Jesus.

You will remember from last week's sermon that doctrine matters. The controversy in this early church gathering in Colossae is, in part, over how unique, how primal Jesus is to be. Jesus is at the center, says Paul. Paul is writing to reestablish Jesus at the center of their doctrine and their life. Place anything else at the center, and it will not last. All the things we desperately substitute will leave us wanting. As one of my mentors used to say, "All success is like cotton candy. It is sweet to the taste, but it will not satisfy the hunger."[4]

We keep moving stuff in and out of the center, changing priorities and anchors, hoping we land on something real. Busy and shallow.

Drive car pool, get the tax stuff together, fix the railing on the porch, order the birthday cake, get the racket restrung, attend another dinner party with people I don't like but need to impress.

"Diet starts next week."

"I know it's wrong, but I can't help flirting back."

"I'm not succeeding as quickly as others—I must be a loser."

"Pour me another. One more glass won't hurt."

"Thanks, I got this at Nieman's."

"Dear God, I'm drowning in shallow water."

Paul has got the man's attention now. He combs his hair back one more time with his fingers, leans in, and listens. He wants to be forgiven. He wants to move from darkness into light. He wants to qualify for a life of meaning and purpose, and he has just learned that he is already qualified. He does not want to drown in shallow water. Somehow he knows that the new life he really wants starts with Jesus.

Lay the other stuff aside; the life you really want starts with Jesus.

NOTES

1. Bruce Manning Metzger, *The New Testament: Its Background, Growth, and Content* (Abingdon Press: Nashville, 1965), 216.

2. Timothy L. Owings, *Drowning in Shallow Water* (Macon, GA: Smyth & Helwys Publishing, 2002), xii.

3. Taken from a Christmas sermon by John R. Claypool titled "The Light of the World," preached December 21, 1975 at Broadway Baptist Church, Fort Worth, TX.

4. John Claypool, often.

3

Getting Clear about Christ

Colossians 1:15-23

Most weeks we skim across the surface of life, bouncing like pinballs from urgent to email, deadline to gridlock, picking up our prescriptions to putting off cleaning the gutters. Our phones beep with reminders to pick up the dry cleaning, buy low-fat groceries, or call about the overage on our cable bill. This pinball existence doesn't seem bad or good; it just is. It is usually not questioned or examined; it just is. (By the way, it occurs to me that some of you may not have ever played pinball—I'm feeling old.)

And then something happens that causes the carnival to stop. All of the lights and sounds and business get unplugged, the room goes dark, and we stare at a different set of questions that lie underneath our concern about when the dry cleaner closes. We have things that intrude on our ordinary circumstances and force us to address the bigger questions that hold life together.

I've had one of those weeks. On Monday morning, the ministry staff met in my office at 8:30, like usual. We brought our coffee cups and sat in a circle and talked about Sunday. "What worked and what didn't?" "Wasn't Diane's baptism moving and important?" "Who was that couple sitting behind the Herndons?" Then, we went around the circle and checked in with each other. "What does your week look like?" "What's the update on the roof on the rental property?" "What time do the youth leave Friday for the ski trip? Does anybody need ski pants?"

This Monday, while we were meeting, we heard a noise outside and the lights in my office flickered off, then on again. Ryan looked out the window of my office and saw a van had crashed into the power pole. We all went to the window. Someone had stopped to check on the accident, and he was calling 911 while frantically trying to wave down a car to stop and help. We grabbed our coats and headed out to help. I went to the window of the van to see if the driver needed help. He wasn't moving. His van had no airbags; I wish I had not seen it. When the ambulance arrived, the firemen waved off the ambulance. They would not be needed.

Slowly and solemnly we made our way back to my office, all of us in a fog. When we settled in to resume our meeting, Ryan said, "So, what really important things were we talking about?"

Two days later, this past Wednesday afternoon, I got a phone call. My best friend from childhood—my next-door neighbor, the one I played with all summer while my little sister tagged along—died in his sleep. He was fifty years old. I'm headed to South Carolina in the morning for his funeral.

Generally speaking, the questions that we ask ourselves stay on the flitting surface. The alarm on the cell phone directs our actions and questions and comings and goings. On most weeks, we ask, "What am I fixing for dinner?" or "Do I have time to get my prescription filled before I need to get her to practice?" Rare is the week when we pull back from the crazy noise and ask big questions like, "What holds life together?"

Most weeks, we weave in and out of the chaos and traffic without asking the big questions. Believe it or not, some people never ask big questions. They just splash through all of the puddles of adulthood without ever stopping to ask important things. For some people, the biggest question of their week is "Who made Rihanna's dress for the Emmy's?" or "Will the college football team ranked number one live up to the hype?"

And as I said, most weeks, most people get by until life starts to unravel. Only then do they ask, "What holds life together?" or "Where do I stand?" or "What is true and ultimate and never-failing?" And, if they have built life around an inferior god, when the storm comes, everything collapses like a house made of sticks.

This is what is at stake in the controversy brewing at the church at Colossae. Members of the Colossian church have competing ideas about what is at the center and what should hold their primary allegiance. We can infer at least two things that are competing for their loyalty, and both are at risk of unseating Jesus as the object of their primary allegiance.

One is Zeus.[1] Yeah, that Zeus. Remember, this is the first century in a strongly Greek-influenced world. Zeus is mentioned a few times in the New Testament, and he is easily worshiped. He is the symbol of all power and virility. He is the god of sky and thunder in Greek mythology, known for his erotic escapades.

He is still worshiped today, just by other names. The worship of power, control, and erotic conquest have not gone away. Zeus is still a real contender for the center of what gives life meaning. In fact, if you look at any trending statistics of church and faith, you could make the case that Zeus worship is winning. The worship of the god of "I'm the boss of me" and "I want to, so I will" is flourishing.

Additionally, first-century Greeks believed that Zeus was at the center of life. Plato tells that his name means, "cause of life always to all things."[2] Walter Burkert, in his book *Greek Religion*, points out that, "Even the gods who are not his natural children address him as Father, and all the gods rise in his presence."[3] For the Greeks, he was the king of the gods who oversaw the universe.

So, Zeus is the god who represents power, control, and erotic conquest, and some in the early church worshiped him above all.

The other contender for the center, for what holds life together, was angels. Paul actually mentions them in the next chapter, "Let no one disqualify you, insisting on self-abasement and worship of angels" (Colossians 2:18, RSV). Apparently, some in the community were insisting on the worship of angels—and who can blame them? Angels are great. White robes, straight teeth, and they make no demands. They float just off the ground of our reality telling pixie dust stories, and their hair stays in place. Who doesn't want to worship angels? Angels bring "good tidings of great joy" (Luke 2:10, KJV). Angels are great.

Besides, Jesus demands things: take up your cross and follow me (Matthew 16:24). You won't hear angels saying things like that. The way of Jesus is the way of suffering and sacrifice, extreme giving and loving, forgiving and redeeming. Jesus does not hover between earth and heaven. Jesus came in the flesh. He lived and spit, walked and demanded, bled and forgave. The way of Jesus is a hard road. It is partnering with God for the hard, redemptive hope of humankind. The way of Jesus involves giving time and money to help the tragic human condition. Angels will pour you a warm bath, and they won't demand a thing.

And don't think angel worship has gone away either. No way. The worship of what sparkles and tickles and fluffs your pillow is very much alive. Worship that does not demand sacrifice and piety is flourishing. I can give you the addresses of some places where people meet regularly for angel worship. They don't call it that of course, but I know that people are having trouble finding parking spaces at some of the arenas where angels are worshiped. It is so seductive. Easy. Beautiful. Comfortable. Warm. I understand why it is thriving. Don't you?

The Colossian church is at a crossroad. They are bickering over doctrine and theology and over who should be at the center of their life together. They believe in Jesus—they have been baptized—but it is hard to give up the worship of Zeus and hard to resist the worship of angels. Besides, all of the rest of the world worships that way. Almost everybody at your law firm, your neighborhood clubhouse, your gym, and your board meeting worships power, control, conquest, or the life of ease. This is why Paul writes this most compelling hymn, this high and exalted and definitive few verses about the supremacy of Christ. To counter all of the noise and seduction of Zeus and angels, Paul preaches and sings. Listen closely for how he answers the challenge of Zeus and angels:

> [Jesus] is the image of the invisible God, the firstborn of all creation *[not like angels—Jesus is visible and human]*; for in him all things in heaven and on earth were created, things visible and invisible, whether thrones or dominions or rulers or powers—all things have been created through him and for him. He himself is before all things, and in him all things hold together *[not Zeus]*. He is the head of the body, the church; he is the beginning, the firstborn from the dead, so that he might come to have first place in everything. For in him all the fullness of God was pleased to dwell, and through him God was pleased to reconcile to himself all things, whether on earth or in heaven, by making peace through the blood of his cross. (vv. 15-20)

Another way to say that last sentence might be, "The fullness of God dwells in Christ. In him, all things hold together." Paul has reached beyond flat prose and appealed with the most lofty, soaring, persuasive language possible to make the case that all things hold together in Christ.

Winston Churchill once said, "Not compressing thought into a reasonable space is sheer laziness."[4] Paul will not be accused of laziness—in these five verses, he has compressed the urgent claim that Jesus is at the center of life.

Beyond the seductions of Zeus and the angels, if you build a life with *anything* other than Christ at the center, it will crumble. Paul is writing with persuasive urgency because he knows the stakes. Eight times in six verses he says "all" or "everything."[5] There is a bold urgency because he knows how much hinges on this one question. "What holds all things together?" Those who worship Zeus will say that power, control, and conquest are at the center. Those who worship angels will say that personal ease and happiness are at the center. Paul says, "The fullness of God dwells in Christ. In him, all things hold together."

In 1923, Hal Luccock wrote a sermon on just that verse, verse 17: "In him, all things hold together."[6] He compares this reality to gravity, the unseen force that holds us to the earth. Without gravity, the world would be thrown into utter chaos, but there is an unseen force that holds our world together.

The unseen power of gravity is not dependent on your belief in it—it just is. Luccock makes the point that the power of Christ holding all things together is likewise just as true. You can harm yourself by not believing in the unseen force of gravity and you can harm yourself by not believing that all things hold together in Christ, but they are both still true whether you believe in them or not.[7]

I know that when you leave here today, most of the messages you'll hear will exalt the virtues of Zeus and the angels. Competing voices are still trying to damage the church. The sermons of Zeus will tell you to compete and take for yourself, that thunder and power and erotic conquest is the place to build your life. Those who preach on behalf of the angels will tell you that your own pleasure and ease are to be sought above all things. But when the silly carnival of our living gets unplugged, we are faced with life's deepest questions. If the questions involve words like, "legacy," "purpose," "calling," or "meaning," you need a bigger god. If they involve "loneliness," "estrangement," "divorce," or "despair," then you need a bigger god. And if "malignant," "fatal," "chronic," or "inoperable" can be used, you need a bigger god.

In the biggest questions of life, Zeus and the angels have nothing to say. They are mute on the questions that matter most. Paul urges us to build life with Christ at the center. *For in him all the fullness of God was pleased to dwell* (v. 19).

Now is the time for response. If you have built your life with any other god at the center, this is a chance for you to say "yes" to building your life around Jesus. You may have done that already and might be looking for a place to be your church home. If you are looking for an imperfect, broken group of people who are trying to follow Jesus at the center of life, this could be it. Bring your life, gifts, and questions, and join us.

NOTES

1. Ralph P. Martin, *Ephesians, Colossians, and Philemon*, Interpretation: A Bible Commentary for Teaching and Preaching (Louisville, KY: Westminster John Knox Press, 1992), 108-09.

2. Plato, *Cratylus*, trans. David Sedley (Cambridge: Cambridge University Press, 2003), 91.

3. Walter Burkert, *Greek Religion* (Cambridge, MA: Harvard University Press, 1985), section III.ii.1.

4. William Manchester and Paul Reid, *The Last Lion: Winston Spencer Churchill, Defender of the Realm, 1940-1965* (New York: Little, Brown and Company, 2012), 30.

5. Timothy L. Owings, *Drowning in Shallow Water* (Macon, GA: Smyth & Helwys Publishing, 2002), 78.

6. Halford E. Luccock, *The Haunted House* (Nashville, TN: Abingdon Press, 1924), 233.

7. Ibid., 232-240.

Getting the Mystery Revealed

Colossians 1:24–2:3

Here is the scene. Paul is sitting in a first-century jail awaiting trial. Prisons were not used as punishment in the first century; instead, they were used as holding cells for trial. Since governors in those days did not have to move to a speedy trial, highly controversial prisoners like Paul might sit for a while. So here's Paul, likely to be underground in a rock jail cell waiting for his day in court. A manhole-like opening above is the only contact with the outside world, and every now and then someone lowers food, but very seldom does anyone clean out this place that smells terrible for obvious reasons on which I will not elaborate.[1] Today, he is not worried about the filth and the stink. Like most pastors, he is deeply concerned for the people in his care. To use his words, *For this I toil* (v. 29).

On this day, his heart is burdened for the believers of Colossae, and he is in the middle of writing them a letter to be read in their church. He has finished writing the greeting, he's addressed the problem of their controversy, and he's just written an inspired and soaring hymn about the supremacy of Christ. The hymn, which we read last week, begins:

> He is the image of the invisible God,
> the first-born of all creation;
> for in him all things were created,
> in heaven and on earth, visible and invisible…(1:15-16, RSV)

These high and grand claims about the singular preeminence of Christ, this elevated call to worship only the Christ: he's finished writing that. But now he's stuck.

He knows that worship alone is not enough. Bowing and worshiping before the great Christ is but one step toward Christian maturity. How to explain the life of faith that will move this congregation to mature living? This is what he considers as he paces his small cell.

Paul spends a few verses explaining why he has never been to visit them. It may sound a bit defensive, but some of the folks at the church have probably been critical of the fact that the apostle has never seen fit to attend even one of their services.

Well, Paul would love to visit the good people of Colossae, but he's stuck in a prison cell right now. He'd especially like to see them face-to-face because he knows of the controversy that is threatening to tear this congregation apart. Some want to worship Zeus; some want to worship angels; some are arguing that Jesus should not hold the singular preeminent place in their worship and devotion. He would love to have this conversation in person, but the Roman jail is forcing him to address them by letter.

He sits in the stink and tries to think of just the right words. The gorgeous hymn just poured out of him as though he were taking dictation, the words soaring and inspired. But now, he is trying to think of just the right thing to write that might inspire them to a life of devotion. He wants the Colossians to grow into mature Christ followers but he can't find the words.

He is stuck on a timeless problem with preaching and writing: he wants to describe the great benefits of following a life of devotion, to describe the riches found in the way of pious reflection, but badness is always easier to describe than goodness. Evil is always easier to describe than piety. English Professor Ralph Wood writes that the novelist P. D. James has this same problem:

> James confesses, regretfully, that evil is much easier to depict than good. A stolen cache, a slashed throat, a slandered reputation—these all attract immediate interest. Goodness, by contrast, is enormously difficult to give vibrant fictional life. Precisely because it is often quiet and undramatic, James explains, charity is hard to make artistically compelling.[2]

How will Paul begin to guide them toward a life of devotion and the incredible gift of that life? It is as near to them as breath, but it is so hard to describe.

For all of salvation history, the Israelite people have been waiting on the Messiah. With only a few biblical examples of theophany—that is, God manifesting—God has been acting in history as the Mysterious Other, the

Great Mystery who moves the stars and the planets but who does not show up often. And now, with the coming of Christ into the world, the mystery is revealed. God has a face. We know the values, priorities, and heartbeat of God because the person of Jesus has walked, taught, lived, loved, forgiven, and suffered among us. The Mystery is revealed. And by the gift of the Holy Spirit, Christ is in you.

Imagine, for all of Jewish history, families had been praying and lighting candles, passing along the heritage of the faith and asking for the coming Messiah. They have told the story of Moses asking to see the face of God, and God showing him only the back of the robe. And now, the Mystery is revealed, Christ abides in you! The God that all of human history has been yearning to see now abides in you. In prayer and private devotion, in worship and holy conversations, you have access to—even daily relationship with—the God of history. You can grow into Christian maturity by giving attention to the remarkable gift of Mystery revealed.

How does Paul even begin to put that into words? There is so much at stake. Finally, Paul smooths out his small piece of papyrus and continues to write. He has already jotted down words about his suffering and now continues with the letter:

> ...to make the word of God fully known, the mystery that has been hidden throughout the ages and generations but has now been revealed to his saints. To them God chose to make known how great among the Gentiles are the riches of the glory of this mystery, which is Christ in you, the hope of glory. It is he whom we proclaim, warning everyone and teaching everyone in all wisdom, so that we may present everyone mature in Christ.... that they may have all the riches of assured understanding and have the knowledge of God's mystery, that is, Christ himself, in whom are hidden all the treasures of wisdom and knowledge. (1:25-28, 2:2-3)

The knowledge of God's mystery and the treasures of wisdom and knowledge are yours because of Christ in you.

Do you see the seemingly hopeless task? Everyone is seeking meaning. There is a never-ending search for wisdom and knowledge, and yet it is ours to attain without any more frantic searching. Be quiet; be still. In solitude and community, worship and prayer, you can find Christ alive in you and access all the treasures of wisdom and inner peace.

There is a great rabbinic story of a poor rabbi who lived in the city of Krakow. He lived on the street of the Lost Angel, in the last hovel on that street, with his wife and four children. Since he was so poor, he dreamed every night about getting rich, and one night he dreamed about a treasure underneath a bridge in the city of Warsaw. So he woke up and excitedly told his wife about the dream and packed up to make the journey to find his treasure. After a long journey, he found it—the bridge was just like it was in his dream, except there was a guard. Tired from his journey, he found a place in the bushes to go to sleep, and when he woke up, the guard heard the rattling of the bushes and came up to confront him, "What are you doing here?" The simple man would not lie. He told the guard about his dream and that he dreamed that underneath that bridge was a great treasure and that he wanted to be rich. The guard said, "That is strange! Just last night I, too, had a dream about hidden treasure, but it was just a dream, so it couldn't be true." He said that he dreamed that in the city of Krakow, on the street of the Lost Angel, in the last hovel on that street, where lives a rabbi and his wife and four children, there is buried, behind the fireplace, a treasure. So the rabbi raced back—the long journey—went to his home, moved away the fireplace, dug underneath, found the treasure, and lived happily ever after.

How will Paul ever convince the people of Colossae that what they most want in the world is already theirs?

> *That they may have all the riches of assured understanding and have the knowledge of God's mystery, that is, Christ himself, in whom are hidden all the treasures of wisdom and knowledge.* (2:2-3)

The mystery is revealed and Christ dwells within you.

There is a wonderful Zen saying: "Riding on an ox, looking for an ox." Wouldn't you feel foolish knowing that you were riding on an ox, looking for an ox?"

I think that is what Paul is trying to get through to them. *The treasures of wisdom and knowledge* are not out there; they are in here. Your pursuit of a better address, a faster car, a more fashionable handbag; your fearful accumulations of stocks and property and other holdings; your child's academic success, your grandchild's athletic success, your own career success; all of the things out there that you chase will never quiet the storm.

The only thing that will make the fear go away is the Mystery revealed, Christ alive within you. Only in the quiet of worship and devotion can you know that the God of the universe loves you. Paying attention to your soul is the only way that you can ever find out that you are accepted and loved, and none of it is earned. You can't earn enough, succeed enough, get pretty enough, or be popular enough to make the fear go away. What you are looking for out there can only be found in here.

You are riding on an ox, looking for an ox. You are traveling from Krakow to Warsaw, and the treasure is buried in Krakow. But this is how Paul chose to write it on that little scrap of papyrus:

> ... *the riches of the glory of this mystery, which is Christ in you, the hope of glory.* (1:27)

The invitation of God is an invitation to discipleship. We gather to worship each Sunday, and some of you may choose to join this congregation because you have been worshiping with us for some time. You feel that now is the time to join this family of believers. I hope you do. But worship is only part of what it means to be a Christ follower. We are also developing disciples, devoting ourselves to the life of prayer and community and service so that we might live deeper into the truth of Christ within us. If you want to join us in the exploration of what it means to live in trust and not fear, we invite you to say "yes" to Christ within you, and we invite you to join us on the journey.

NOTES

1. Bob Fraser, "Prisons in Paul's World," quoted in "Rejoicing in Your House of Darkness," *A Deeper Treasure* <https://tucker4cc.wordpress.com/2015/06/24/rejoicing-in-your-house-of-darkness/> (accessed 24 January 2018).

2. David L. Bartlett, *What's the Matter with Preaching Today*, ed. Mike Graves (Louisville, KY: Westminster John Knox Press, 2004), 23.

5

Getting from Captivity to the Cross

Colossians 2:4-15

Those closest to me have listened to me complain. As we continue in our nine-week series on Colossians, I have been whining that every passage seems to sound alike. It seems like the theme of every passage and therefore every sermon, has been the centrality and supremacy of Christ. Melissa has been more encouraging than my pastor friend in Macon. Melissa said, "If you are going to be stuck preaching the same theme over and over, that is a good one to be stuck on." She's right. I attended a lecture in Macon this week and I was making this complaint to one of my pastor buddies. His response was, "If your patterns of church attendance are like mine, nobody is going to hear more than three of the nine sermons anyway." Not as encouraging.

But Paul keeps pounding the same message. If you get a multiple-choice question on the book of Colossians, the answer is the one that includes *the centrality and supremacy of Christ.*

Why does Paul keep saying the same thing? As we have discussed, Christ is up against some serious competition for the center of church life in Colossae. A few weeks ago, I preached about some members of the church who wanted to worship Zeus and some who wanted to worship angels. The culture of worship in the first-century Greek world was a culture of worshiping many different entities. If the grain ripened in the field, they said the goddess Ceres was smiling on them. If they heard the sea moaning and roaring, they said Neptune was angry. When their passion ran hot, they gave credit or blame to Venus, the goddess of love. When their armies began to march, they saw it as the activity of the war-god, Mars.[1]

For some, Jesus was just another god to worship—another member of the tribe. But we have also mentioned angel worship, which was part of a set of false beliefs growing in the region. Another heresy grew into what came to be known as Gnosticism. This letter addresses an early skirmish with Gnosticism, but John and others, forty years later, would have to deal with the same heresy after it became a full-blown philosophy. Paul is offering an early answer to the heresy of the Gnostics.

We need to stop, set up the tent, and make camp here for a while. We need to talk about Gnosticism because it shows up here and several more places in the New Testament. Gnosticism begins with two basic assumptions: spirit is good; matter is evil. God is holy, God is spirit, God is pure, and so God must not have anything to do with this flawed, evil, material world. Things of the spirit are good; things of the flesh are bad.

This comes out of Platonic philosophy, and it plays out in one of two ways. One, since spirit is good and matter is bad, and since spirit is eternal and matter is temporary, only the spirit matters at all. You can do what you want to with your body; it has nothing to do with your spirit. So, some would excuse any immorality because the body is separate from the spirit. Others treated the body and matter as evil, sometimes whipping and mutilating their own bodies.

I mentioned that this heresy was born out of the teachings of Plato. When somebody says, "Our relationship is strictly platonic." They are saying that the spirit and body are separate, right? "Our relationship is spiritually connected, but it is not physical in any way." It would also be accurate to say that a one-night stand is a platonic relationship because it separates the physical from the spiritual. My body was involved, but my spirit was not. This is the teaching of the first-century Gnostics. You can do what you want with your body—it's evil and perishing anyway. But, you must preserve a clean and holy and pure spiritual life. Spirit is good; matter is evil.

Stay with me. If spirit is good and matter is evil, then the incarnation is a problem. Gnostic Christians were beginning to promote that Jesus was divine but that Jesus was not fully human. How could he possibly be fully human and divine if matter is evil? Do you see where angel worship creeps in? Angels float between heaven and earth. They are suspended above the nasty, evil world of matter. Gnostics were beginning to teach that Jesus was not fully human but that Jesus was a phantom who was suspended from the grit of our living.

It is one way to reconcile the painful truth of our own sin. If we believe that nurturing the spiritual life is all that matters and that we are free to do what we want with our day-to-day living, then we can reconcile and push aside the nasty choices we keep making as just being temporary, earthly, passing, and having nothing to do with our eternal spiritual life with God.

You and I know some modern-day Gnostics. They often begin stories by saying, "That's fine for you to take that stance, but in the real world...". We know people whose faith seems to have no bearing on their living. I have to keep these stories vague, but a friend of mine has a friend who lives one of the wildest lives I have ever heard of. I think he must have been the model for the movie *The Wolf of Wall Street*. He lives in reckless excess all the time. He cheats in business; he cheats on his wife. From the stories I hear, you would have to cut some footage for his story to get an R rating. And yet, so I'm told, he is an elder in his Presbyterian church. Apparently, his spiritual life and his physical life are separate.

One of the churches I served was in a small town. The same group of men ran everything in town. They ran the Kiwanis, the Rotary, the small country club, the school board, and they were all deacons at the Baptist church. The hospital in the larger town nearby had just hired a new doctor. He bought some land in this small town where our church was and commuted the 12 miles to the hospital. This doctor applied for membership at the nine-hole golf and country club in town. The small club needed members. It was a small and declining town. But the medical doctor was denied membership because he was black. I learned about the decision from a group of these men—just before they walked into a deacons meeting. Apparently they were Gnostics, able to keep their spiritual life and their physical life separate.

I know some men who are only Gnostics when they are more than 200 miles from home. I say "men" because they are the only ones who tell me. Some men live rather integrated lives at home, and when business travel takes them away, they are somehow influenced by Plato. They separate spirit from matter. They justify that the choices they make far from home do not affect their devotion to their wives or their spiritual life. Like the line from a Paul Simon song, "far away my well-lit door,"[2] after 200 miles they become Gnostics, separating matter and spirit.

Paul sees the danger. What will happen if Gnosticism wins the day? Paul must declare two things to be true if he is going to make a first volley on the advancing Gnostic troops. First, he must make clear that Jesus was not some phantom whose feet never touched the ground. Jesus was fully human. Second, he must make clear that sin is not dealt with by bracketing off the life of the flesh from the life of the spirit. We are one. We are both flesh and spirit, and Jesus has come to forgive and redeem both. Our sin is brought with shame to the cross so that it might be transformed and made new. Listen for Paul's answer to the emerging heresy:

> See to it that no one takes you captive through philosophy and empty deceit, according to human tradition, according to the elemental spirits of the universe, and not according to Christ. For in him the whole fullness of deity dwells bodily, and you have come to fullness of life in him, who is the head of every ruler and authority.... And when you were dead in trespasses and the uncircumcision of your flesh, God made you alive together with him, when he forgave us all our trespasses, erasing the record that stood against us with its legal demands. He set it aside, nailing it to the cross. He disarmed the rulers and authorities and made a public example of them, triumphing over them in it. (2:8-10, 13-15)

Christ alone. Here we go again—the centrality and supremacy of Christ. But in this section, he stares in the teeth of the heresy. *In him the whole fullness of deity dwells bodily* (2:9). The feet of Jesus are firmly planted here. And, he has forgiven us all our trespasses, canceled the bond, and nailed it to the cross.

Carlyle Marney once said that many still like for Jesus to hover between heaven and earth because we know that if he ever gets into our grain bin, he will raise Cain with us.

We don't have the luxury of bracketing our living away from our faith. The life of faith intends to penetrate all of who we are. Jesus is fully divine and fully human. We are matter and spirit. We are church and work. We are family and faith. We make vows before heaven and earth. We are called to an integrated life where our spiritual convictions influence our business and our family and our travel and our choices. And when we fail, we can't just ask Plato to put our failures in a separate category. We must allow failure to be nailed to the cross of Christ, where forgiveness and triumph happen.

The invitation today is for those who want forgiveness and a new start and for those who want to move a step closer to living the integrated life of faith. Nobody here does it perfectly but we are a church dedicated to trying. We are trying to learn and live the life of faith—what the early church called the Way. It is best done in community, and we invite you to join us.

Join your imperfect life with ours, and in community, we will try to follow the Way together.

NOTES

1. W. Randall Lolley, "Colossians: A Crown and a Head for It," a sermon preached at First Baptist Church, Greensboro, NC, June 30, 1996.
2. Paul Simon, "You Can Call Me Al," *Graceland*, 1986, Warner Bros. Records.

6

Getting Free from the World to Make a Difference

Colossians 2:16–3:4

In the first century, in what is modern day Turkey, about 300 miles east of Ephesus, there were three ancient cities that were clustered together in the Lycus River Valley. The smallest of the three was Colossae. The river valley made for great pastureland and the woolen industry flourished in the tri-city area. Commerce was good, people came in and out of the region, and some of that traffic brought the Christian gospel into the city of Colossae. Thus, a church was formed.

The young church was struggling with how to be Christ followers in this culture of competing gods. The good news of Jesus Christ did not go into a region without religion, just one without Christianity. Some were worshiping the Greek gods: Zeus, Aphrodite, and others. Some were influenced by the teachings of Plato and the heretical doctrine of what would become Gnosticism. As we saw last week, Gnosticism is the belief that matter, body, and flesh are bad; that spirit, soul, and God are good; and that they should be kept separate.

Gnosticism is not a religion but a philosophy that was gaining traction within Christianity and taking one of two forms. Some interpreted the philosophy to say that if matter is bad and spirit is good, I can do whatever pleasure seeking that I want with my body because my spirit is unaffected. Others interpreted the philosophy to mean that, if the body is bad, then it should be treated as base and nasty and evil. Apparently some in the church at Colossae had this very idea—that the body is evil and so the "really pious, the really holy" in the group should treat their bodies with disdain.

They would eat very little, abstain from intimacy, and some might have even engaged in some self-mutilation just to show how holy and pious they were. Welts, apparently, were the marks of a committed Christian.

They also lived for the holy days of festivals, like the new moon and the Sabbath. Here's why. They would, by some kind of mystical initiation, worship in the vision of the angelic realm on these holy days—suspended, they believed, above the nasty physical world.[1] They were the real holy ones, the self-appointed special group. They were doing so many impressive and obvious things to show how devout they were.

So what is a young, sincere Christian to do? There is this pressure from the cool kids. If you really want to show your commitment, you will abuse your body and seek special religious experiences. You will be shunned or disqualified if you don't. There are special things that the special group does and, more importantly, there are things that the really committed ones don't do—*Do not handle, Do not taste, Do not touch* (2:21).

As we have been learning together, Paul is writing this early church to correct heresy and get these early Christians back on track. Remember, "the centrality and supremacy of Christ" is his loud and recurring theme, which he said in response to the group insisting on a rigid religion. Let's hear Paul's response from the J. B. Phillips translation:

> In view of these tremendous facts, don't let anyone worry you by criticizing what you eat or drink, or what holy days you ought to observe, or bothering you over new moons or sabbaths. All these things have at most only a symbolical value: the solid fact is Christ. Nor let any man cheat you of your joy in Christ by persuading you to make yourselves "humble" and fall down and worship angels. Such a man, inflated by an unspiritual imagination, is pushing his way into matters he knows nothing about, and in his cleverness forgetting his head. It is from the head alone that the body, by natural channels, is nourished and built up and grows according to God's laws of growth.
>
> So if, through your faith in Christ, you are dead to the principles of this world's life, why, as if you were still part and parcel of this worldwide system, do you take the slightest notice of these purely human prohibitions—"Don't touch this," "Don't taste that" and "Don't handle the other"? "This," "that" and "the other" will all pass away after use! I know that these regulations look wise with their self-inspired efforts at worship, their policy of self-humbling, and their studied neglect of the

body. But in actual practice they do honor, not to God, but to man's own pride.

Well Paul, tell us what you really think.

So how in the world can a bunch of self-mutilating Gnostics have anything to do with us? We are so distant from that time. We are so distant from those nouns. So much of the richness of Scripture is that the nouns change over time but the human action, the verbs, never change. We really do struggle with the same issues.

I attended a wonderful lecture this week by Anna Carter Florence, who teaches preaching at Columbia Theological Seminary here in Atlanta. She is the one who has made me more sensitive to nouns and verbs in Holy Scripture. She points out that many of the ancient nouns are different from our lives, so they distance us from the setting of Scripture. We don't talk much of *new moons* and *elemental spirits*, and some translating is needed to bridge the cultural gap.

But the verbs are another matter. The verbs do not need translating; we understand them all too well. Listen to a few of the verbs given to the group of self-appointed pious people: "pass judgment," *disqualify*, "taking his stand," *puffed up*. There is no distance at all between those verbs and what we see from the self-appointed pious community today.

There are some areas of the modern Christian church where self-appointed piety is thriving—where the good news of the Christian gospel is reduced to what you cannot do or say or eat or drink or wear. There are communities that major in issues of a "puffed up piety" and make it central to the life of faith lived out among them.

For instance, I'm really not that old, really—and when I was in seminary, a friend of mine had a part-time youth ministry position in seminary like I did. He came to class one Monday and told us that he had been fired. He was fired because he took the youth group to the lake and allowed "mixed bathing." Some of you recognize that old term, and others of you need to know that it is not nearly as naughty as it sounds. He allowed the boys and girls in his youth group to swim together in the lake—"mixed bathing" was the name of the sin that disqualified him. He didn't even know he was breaking one of the pious rules.

Maybe I have some scars from time spent with the outwardly pious. When I was in college, I was a Christianity major headed to seminary. And I was a member of a social fraternity. There was a group of guys, also studying for ministry, who would come to our upper-level Christianity classes, set their hard Samsonite briefcases on the desks, unsnap them, pull out their Scofield Bibles, plop them on the desks, and never speak to me. I was in a fraternity. I was not as pious. I did not qualify.

We want to qualify. Sincere people will adopt silly behaviors just to qualify. Years ago, I took my youth group to a big youth event. I remember seeing a group of boys from another youth group who were walking together. They all looked alike. Each had on blue jeans, flip-flops, hats with the bill turned way in and big fish hooks clipped to the bill—they were fishers of men. Each wore a different Christian t-shirt with a clever slogan. Witness wear was youth-group cool. They were the pious ones. "They will know we are Christians by our T-shirts." I suppose nobody wanted to be disqualified.

We may too easily identify "passing judgment," "taking a stand," and "disqualifying" with the ultraconservative wing of the church family. But, it is a sin of the left as well. I was talking with a buddy who was Minister of Education at a more liberal church in North Carolina. I knew of another liberal Baptist church in his town, so I asked how the cultures of the two churches were alike and different. Keep in mind: being the most liberal Baptist church is like being the tallest building in Tupelo, Mississippi. But I asked, "How are they alike and different? What distinguishes one church from the other?" He stammered a moment and then said, "I'll answer you as a Christian educator. At the other church, the children may or may not be taught John 3:16, but they will all know how to recycle." You can bet that church would disqualify any Christians who did not recycle.

I agree with what Tim Owings says about this behavior when he says,

> Rigid religion is dangerous because it suggests—oh so carefully—that if you get your religion right, your behavior right, your actions right, then, you have got God right. God is right where you want God to be: on your side.[2]

If we fill up our Christian lives with the clutter of our past and the clutter of all the religious rules—there may be no space or freedom to worship and follow the risen Christ. Hear Paul declare another, better way:

> If then you have been raised with Christ, seek the things that are above, where Christ is, seated at the right hand of God. Set your minds on things that are above, not on things that are on earth. For you have died, and your life is hid with Christ in God. When Christ who is your life appears, then you also will appear with him in glory. (3:1-4, ESV)

Let's look at some verbs again: *have been raised, seek, set your minds, appears, will appear.* Aren't these verbs so much better than those in the earlier list?

We do not want new believers, or any of us, to have a distorted faith that centers on passing judgment, taking stands, and disqualifying others. We want for them and the rest of our fellowship what Paul has turned us toward. We want the baptized community to seek the things set above, to set our minds on the things that are above, and to live into the fullness of the glory of Christ.

It is important to live with high ethical standards and with deep commitment to moral principles, but Paul knows that a religion that is centered on forbidden behaviors and passing judgment on others will turn sick in a hurry. We are called to follow a religion that is centered in Christ. We were created to live in abundant relationship with God and with others. Get free; *you have been raised with Christ, seek the things that are above, where Christ is…* (3:1).

Have you ever been around someone who really lived in that free space where grace grows? Have you been around someone who lives not by the rules imposed by the tribe but lives seeking the things that are above and focusing on the spectacular freedom of it? They are my heroes. They live with buoyancy and delight.

In our baptism services, our new believers declare, "Jesus is Lord," are buried with Christ, then are raised with Christ to seek the things that are above. Perhaps today is the day when you want to come forward and say that it is time for you to make that same decision. Perhaps this is the day for you to join this church and join this group of Christians who are reading and worshiping and trying to follow the faith passed onto us. We would welcome you. Perhaps it is time to reestablish Christ at the center and recommit to seeking things that are above.

NOTES

1. Francis W. Beare, "The Epistle to Colossians: Exegesis," *The Interpreter's Bible*, Vol. 11 (Nashville: Abingdon Press, 1955), 204.

2. Timothy L. Owings, *Drowning in Shallow Water: The Hope of Colossians for Today's Culture* (Macon, GA: Smyth & Helwys Publishing, 2002), 35.

Getting Dressed for Abundant Living

Colossians 3:5-17

I left last week's service feeling so good. The week before, I complained about how every sermon was starting to sound alike. Every part of Colossians was Paul taking one more stab at "the centrality and supremacy of Christ." But last week was different. The men's choir was spectacular. We witnessed a baptism. It was a great day. We also got to talk about something other than the centrality and supremacy of Christ. We talked about rigid religion and how we can get sidetracked away from the life of grace by worrying too much about the rules—what is okay to eat or drink or wear. It was liberating. I left feeling great.

Then, I got to today's message, read the hard and indicting words, and wished I could go back to preaching the centrality and supremacy of Christ. And I really miss last week's message about us being free from the rules of a rigid religion. Today's message is hard.

The impact is not unlike Jesus' Sermon on the Mount. Remember, Jesus had been going all through the countryside breaking the rules of the religious tradition. He healed on the Sabbath and allowed his disciples to pick grain on the Sabbath. The religiously rigid in his day were furious. They were counting out how many steps you could take on the Sabbath before it was considered working. I mean, you needed to have enough steps to get to the bathroom and back but too many steps and well, you might as well have gone on out in the field and worked all day.

Jesus reacts against the legalism, and the disciples are beginning to recline into this new freedom from the rules. Then Jesus speaks: You have heard it said, do not murder, but I say unto you, do not even hate that much.... You have heard it said, do not commit adultery, but I say unto you, do not even look at a woman like that (Matthew 5:21-22, 27-28) He is not lowering expectations when freeing us from the law; he is ratcheting them up.

Paul does the same thing here. Before I read the hard words written to the church at Colossae, I need to warn you. Paul's words will indict you, too, if you listen too closely. If you really listen, you will squirm a little in your seat. We could avoid this. I could chase the scholarly debates and keep this from getting in our stuff.

For instance, one commentary says, "Did Colossians have a problem in this particular area? Was Paul being corrective or preventative?"[1] See, I could chase what was going on in that particular church and keep us distanced. I could talk about the scholarly suggestion that there were inappropriate intimate relationships within that church community and that it was one of the things that might tear apart this fellowship. I could chase a counterargument—and I'm tempted, because you and I are not going to like the implications of this reading if we put ourselves in Paul's words instead of the Colossians. Sermons are easier to hear when I talk about "them" and not "us."

And let me say more about that. One of the great privileges of pastoral ministry is that I hear some of your secrets. Some of you might think that when I preach a passage like this, that I am looking straight at you and betraying your secret. I am not. I would never betray your secret—it is just that because I hear your stories, I am one of the few people in the room who knows that everyone here is keeping secrets. Some of them I know. The ones that matter most are the ones you know.

The indicting part of the letter I'm about to read implicated everyone in the first-century house church when Epaphras read it out loud, and it will implicate everybody in here too because we all have secrets. Paul is addressing the Colossians's sin and ours.

Two more warnings before I read it. First is the recognition that each of us is guilty of some part of this list. Paul clearly says, *These are the ways you also once followed, when you living that life* (3:7). We have all lived in them. But just because we are all guilty, don't hear the list and try to grade yourself on the curve. Don't just recline and say, "Well, nobody's perfect," because Paul also says, *On account of these the wrath of God is coming* (3:6). Whenever we make people into objects, God is angry.

Are you ready? This is the list. These are the offenses that are as ancient as a first-century house church in Colossae and as recent as your current Internet search history. Listen if you dare:

> Put to death therefore what is earthly in you: fornication, impurity, passion, evil desire, and covetousness [*that is, wanting other people's stuff*], which is idolatry. On account of these the wrath of God is coming. In these you once walked, when you lived in them. But now put them all away: anger, wrath, malice, slander, and foul talk from your mouth. Do not lie to one another, seeing that you have put off the old nature with its practices… (3:5-9, paraphrase)

If we had ears to hear, the best sermon might be reading this for twenty minutes until we felt the "Fifty Shades" of shame and wanted to be made new.

Do you see? The Gnostics were saying that the body is evil; therefore, we should deprive it and self-mutilate to show how pious we are, to which Paul said, "That's ridiculous." Then, just as we thought we had a hall pass, Paul says, "It's tougher than that. Here's what I want you to do with the physical world you inhabit: put away fornication, impurity, passion, evil desire, and covetousness" (v. 5).

The worship of any appetite is another way that we put something other than Jesus in the center of our lives. And, we all worship something. We all have a god.

I have two newspaper angels in this congregation. The first angel will not surprise you; it is Edie Whitaker. When Edie reads something in the paper that has anything to do with someone connected to Second-Ponce, she cuts it out and puts it on my desk. My other newspaper angel will surprise you—it is Jere Goldsmith. Jere cuts out articles from the *Wall Street Journal* that touch on religious issues. Jere as an angel—I know, unlikely.

A few weeks ago, he gave me an article about Tim Keller, the popular New York City pastor of Redeemer Presbyterian Church. Mr. Keller makes just this point in his *Wall Street Journal* interview. He suggests that we all worship some god, some appetite—and I agree.

> "Everyone has a God, everyone has a way of salvation, we just don't use the term," he says. "St. Augustine would say: What makes you what you really are is what you love the most." Mr. Keller adds that he likes "to show secular people that they're not quite as unreligious as they think. They're putting their hopes in something, and they're living for it." For ambitious, driven New Yorkers, it's often a career, he says. "I try to tell people: The only reason you're laying yourself out like this is because you're not really just working. This is very much your religion."[2]

Some of us worship the appetite of accumulation and success and getting more than other people get. Covetousness is the biblical word—wanting what others have. For some, the appetite is so strong that it becomes an unhealthy religious pursuit. Relationships become a way of getting what we want. The other appetite that destroys is the pursuit of physical pleasure that treats people as objects—it is another satisfaction of appetite that uses relationships as a way to get what I want. And we are all guilty. Paul says,

> Put to death therefore what is earthly in you: fornication, impurity, passion, evil desire, and covetousness, which is idolatry. On account of these the wrath of God is coming. (3:5-6, RSV)

Is there any hope? Paul says, "Yes, put this on! You must change clothes. Take off what you have been wearing and put this on instead."

> As God's chosen ones, holy and beloved, clothe yourselves with compassion, kindness, humility, meekness, and patience. Bear with one another and, if anyone has a complaint against another, forgive each other; just as the Lord has forgiven you, so you also must forgive. Above all, clothe yourselves with love, which binds everything together in perfect harmony. And let the peace of Christ rule in your hearts, to which indeed you were called in the one body. And be thankful. Let the word of Christ dwell in you richly; teach and admonish one another in all wisdom; and with gratitude in your hearts sing psalms, hymns, and spiritual songs to God. And whatever you do, in word or deed, do everything in the name of the Lord Jesus, giving thanks to God the Father through him. (3:12-17)

This is about as straightforward as it gets. I wish I could put this medicine in some Jell-O to make it easier to take, but Paul is just ruthless on this one. If you are pursing relationships for your own gain and pleasure, if you are treating people like things and things like treasures, you need to stop. *On account of these, the wrath of God is coming* (v. 6).

You know by now that my image of God is one of creative goodness. You know that I am motivated to this work because I have experienced so much of God's grace and provision and unyielding love. You know how much I love preaching the wide expanse of God's grace in the world. But some texts just indict us. We must stand together under the terrible nearness of God and hear the hard words. But we know that one movement of

God's love is like a loving parent. A loving parent who sees a child running toward an open fire will yell "stop" because the parent knows the pain that that child is running toward. God's love also yells "stop" if we are doing destructive things.

Paul is not playing around here. You are running into fire, and Paul is sternly yelling at us to stop. Stop treating others as means of satisfying your appetites. Take that outfit off and put on this one: compassion, kindness, lowliness, meekness, patience, forbearance, forgiveness. And above all these, put on love, which binds everything together in perfect harmony. This is the way of abundant life.

Interestingly, this very personal work of renewal is also the work of community. We do this together. We pray for each other and hold each other accountable and help each other assemble new outfits with the new accessories of compassion and kindness, forbearance and forgiveness.

Many of these pronouns in today's Scripture are in the plural: "*you* put to death," "*you* must get rid of all such things," "*you* do not lie." In Greek the "*you*" is plural. Translated into standard, proper Southern English, it is "y'all."

Y'all help each other get dressed. Y'all keep each other away from destructive places and eroding habits. Y'all come together to read and study and sing and worship. Y'all join the church and get involved in Sunday school and study and push and ask and pray. Y'all develop soul friendships here, people whom you can trust with the unfinished parts. Y'all hear each other's confessions, and y'all help each other rebuild. This is the work of the church. Y'all help each other get dressed for abundant living.

NOTES

1. Timothy L. Owings, *Drowning in Shallow Water: The Hope of Colossians for Today's Culture* (Macon, GA: Smyth & Helwys Publishing), 136

2. Kate Bachelder, "God Isn't Dead in Gotham," The Weekend Interview with Timothy Keller, *The Wall Street Journal* (20-21 December 2014), A13.

8

Getting Relationships in Order

Colossians 3:18–4:1

Wives, be subject to your husbands.... Slaves, obey your earthly masters (vv. 18, 20). As T. J. Boyle said this week, "You did not plan your vacation well. This would have been a good week to ask Charles to preach." No kidding.

As you know, I have been asked to write a book of sermons on Colossians, and I can't skip any part of the letter. The book must cover the whole of Colossians. Nine sermons on four chapters are surely going to cover it. The idea is that once it is published, other preachers can pull down the volume and see how someone else preached the text they are preaching this week. This will be the least-read chapter in the book. Nobody who has a choice is preaching this section. A woman pastor is not likely to choose "Wives be subject to your husbands." A married male pastor is aware that any mishandling of the subject means two weeks on the couch. Most preachers are going to look for something in Exodus to preach this week.

But here we go. This is what we signed up for, so let's recap.

The young church at Colossae is troubled. They are disagreeing about what to believe. In a culture of multiple gods being worshiped, some within the church were treating Jesus as another good option rather than the central truth of our existence. Also, the church is dealing with the growing influence of Gnostic philosophy. The Gnostics believe that there are two realities—spirit and matter. God and spirit are good. Flesh and matter are bad. So they treated their bodies as evil, and some went as far as self-mutilation. They treated their faith as something to connect to way up in the spiritual realm away from this earthly living. They would live for the holy festivals where they could worship themselves up off the ground and commune with a mystical, spiritual faith that hung somewhere between earth and heaven.

Paul, the pastor, writes the Colossians to get this young church back on track. In the first chapters he pounds on the same message over and over and over. It is the central message, and if you don't get this one right, the rest of the faith doesn't make much sense. Jesus is not just another god in the pantheon, Jesus is supremely God—"For in him all the fullness of God was pleased to dwell, and through him God was pleased to reconcile to himself all things…" (1:19-20).

Then Paul takes on the Gnostics. He assures us that Jesus came in the flesh. Body and spirit are together: "For in him the whole fullness of deity dwells bodily…" (2:9). He addresses Gnosticism by saying that we are not to divide life into two parts—spirit and body—and live in the legalism of dietary restrictions and other ways of shaming the body. "Do not let anyone disqualify you, insisting on self-abasement and worship of angels" (2:18).

And then, as the saying goes, Paul stops preaching and goes to meddling. We were all shouting "Amen," "Hallelujah" when the first chapters sang songs of the exalted Christ—but then, last week, Paul started meddling. The response to Gnostic dualism was not that we should separate body and spirit, but we should "put on the new self" (3:10). We should clothe ourselves with purity and give up the immoral, impure ways we have been living.

And today, now that Paul has us by the throat, he is not letting go. Paul wants this faith in Jesus Christ to affect our relationships. If the fullness of God dwells bodily in Jesus, then spirit and matter are connected. Faith and living are tied together. You can't just wait for a festival and worship yourself into an ecstatic, mystical frenzy. This faith must affect your living. And there is an order, a progression to the effect it ought to have. First, as we saw last week, it ought to affect your most private behavior. Your most intimate relationships should be conducted as though your life has been changed. Give up the immoral and impure and put on a new set of clothes.

Today's Scripture opens the circle a bit wider. It deals with how the life of faith should impact the relationships at home. If you are a changed follower of Christ, then it ought to show up in the way you conduct your private morality and in the way you relate to those at home: *Wives, be subject to your husbands, as is fitting in the Lord. Husbands, love your wives and never treat them harshly* (vv. 18-19). Each of these relationships has a balanced mutuality. All of these household relationships are spoken of in pairs. Wives, husbands. Children, parents. Slaves, masters. There is a responsibility of behavior in all of our household relationships.

But if we are going to deal with this honestly, we can't avoid the hard stuff. We have to ask the question that scholar Ben Witherington asked, "Was Paul a Pro-Slavery Chauvinist?"[1] After all, this text has been a favorite of slavery advocates and chauvinists for years. *Slaves, obey your masters* does not sound like the words of a guy who thinks slavery is morally wrong (v. 22). *Wives, obey your husbands* does not sound like a guy who is on the board of the National Organization of Women (v. 18).

The important cultural distinction here is that Paul does not address social ethics at all. Christian ethics were personal. Christians in Paul's day were not citizens with responsibility in and for government. Social order was not something that Christians could decide or change. Paul and the early Christians were subjects. The only reach of ethics was personal and relational.

That said, we also can't just gloss over first-century slavery. Slavery in the New Testament was not a kinder, gentler slavery. As Richard Seller says, "The lot of bad slaves was to be beaten and that of good slaves was to internalize the constant threat of a beating."[2] Slavery was evil then, too. It is just that the Christian had no reach into social ethics. Paul is not arguing for slavery or endorsing it. It just is—subjects have no voice in the structure of society. We have it tougher today. In our society, we do shape civic life. We do have power over the social structure.[3]

Government workers, governors, judges, and legislators are part of our congregation. We also vote. We do have a responsibility for our Christian ethics to inform how the marginalized of society are treated. Our understanding of the gospel had better inform how we structure our civic life. We can influence how "the least of these" get treated. Paul could not. It would not even have been in his wildest thoughts to think of addressing the social evil of his day. Paul's circle of morality is smaller than ours. Paul is asking a more personal question. How will your Christian faith make a difference in your relationships at home?

Part of the way we misuse this text is to underline the wrong lines. Historically, this Scripture has been misused to argue for how others ought to behave, keeping my behavior unchallenged. Our temptation is to skip every other line so we can straighten up those around us. I like to underline these verses: *Wives, be subject to your husbands; Children, obey your parents* (vv. 18; 20). Praise God we no longer have slavery—but I also want those who work for me to obey and work with singleness of heart.

If my staff would just do what I want them to do, if my children would just do what I want them to do, if Melissa would just be subject to me like the Holy Book clearly says, then my life would be great. (I may end up on the sofa yet.)

Our misuse of this Scripture—to get others to line up and do what I want them to do for my pleasure and satisfaction—is exactly opposite of its intent. Paul is saying that the Christian life should impact your relationships and that the selfless, loving, forgiving model of Christ should be the model of our primary relationships. To take this Scripture and turn it into a weapon for getting others to straighten up is a perversion of its intent.

Dehumanizing others while waving the Bible is simply wrong. Listen to this entry from an online blog. This woman is a self-proclaimed submissive wife. She writes in her blog:

> Well here I am up at 6:40 AM! I just put the kids on the school bus and instead of going back to sleep, I am up, showered, and ready to start my day! Alex gave me quite a bit of extra chores to do today since I had been lazy and did not finish all of them yesterday prior to him coming home. He had a special night planned for us, but since I wasn't finished with my chores by the time he got home, we weren't able to go due to the fact that I was still doing them.
>
> I was punished last night for sleeping in and not going to the doctor. Alex said that he would punish me for not completing my chores by giving me extra to do today. My punishment was kind of mild compared to the one I received for lying to him! When he got home, go figure I had just sat down to take a quick break and I didn't see him pull into the driveway. I like to watch *All My Children*, and Alex doesn't mind as long as it doesn't interfere with my duties.[4]

Apparently, her husband backed her in a corner and yelled some Colossians at her. That is about as sick and far from the passage's intent as I can imagine.

Have you seen the scene in the movie *12 Years a Slave*[5] when the plantation owner quotes Scripture before whipping his slave? He opens his Bible and reads from Luke, *And that servant, which knew his lord's will, and prepared not himself, neither did according to his will, shall be beaten with many stripes* (Luke 12:47, KJV). He then shuts the Bible and says, "That's Scripture."

Whenever we use the Bible to diminish the humanity of another, whenever we start quoting to get somebody else to line up, we are distorting Scripture at best and participating in pure evil at worst.

That is not the nature of these verses. For their day, this letter empowered those with little power. In this section of Colossians, wives are empowered with choice, and slaves are given inheritance. There is a mutual obligation in these verses that moves us closer to the divine hope—not an over/under quality that moves us toward an imprisoned relationship. Paul is not giving us a weapon. Paul is giving us a challenge—to look at the verses that shine light on us. The challenge is to grow into letting the model of Christ influence my living. It is much harder if I turn these lines onto myself instead of others, if I underline the other verses:

Husbands, love your wives and never treat them harshly (3:19).

Fathers, do not provoke your children, or they may lose heart (3:21).

Bosses, treat those who work for you justly and fairly.

Now, I have work to do.

The Gnostics wanted to keep the spiritual life separate from the physical life. But Paul says if the fullness of God dwells bodily in Jesus, then spirit and matter are connected. Faith and living are tied together. When you put on the new clothes of compassion, forgiveness, love, and forbearance, it ought to affect those around you. Those in your home should see a difference. Faith and your dinner table are connected. Your faith should inform how you correct your children. Children, your faith should show up in how you speak to your parents. Your faith and how you treat your spouse are connected.

When we hear Paul's words about relationships, we should never say, "You sure told them." We should say, "Ouch. Now I have work to do."

We are working on this Christian life together. If you have not said, "yes" to the life of faith, we invite you to do so today and begin your journey with us. If you are searching for a faith community to learn and grow and live with, we invite you to join this church today and work with us as a partner in the enterprise of Christ. For all of us, consider how the claim of Christ should make a difference in your relationships, and use this time of decision to move your own life closer to God's hope for you.

NOTES

1. Ben Witherington III, "Was Paul a Pro-Slavery Chauvinist? Making Sense of Paul's Seemingly Mixed Moral Message," *B Rev* 20/2 (2004).

2. Richard Seller, *Narratives of the Sufferings of Richard Seller: A Member of the Religious Society of Friends, in Support of Their Testimony Against War* (London: Forgotten Books, 1832), quoted in Andrew Lincoln, *Ephesians*, WBC 42 (Dallas, TX: Word, 1990), 421.

3. Francis W. Beare, "The Epistle to the Colossians: Exegesis," *The Interpreters Bible*, Vol. 11 (Nashville, TN: Abingdon Press, 1955), 223.

4. "Samantha's Life as a Submissive Wife," Samanthaslife-spanked.blogspot.com, 14 September 2007 (accessed 02 October 2017).

5. John Ridley, 12 Years a Slave, DVD, directed by Steve McQueen (Los Angeles: Fox Searchlight, 2013).

9

Getting a Little Help from My Friends

Colossians 4:2-18

We have come to the end of our time in Colossians. You are officially the most currently informed congregation on the planet regarding the letter to the Colossians. You may not be well informed, but you are the most currently informed. You may feel like the farmer in the story I read this week. This was in a book written in 1936. A devout farmer had just, like you, listened to a long series of sermons on the Book of Colossians. At the end of the series the old farmer said, "The Colossians… must have been very clever folk. If, as we're told, the epistle was just a letter written to be read to them, I suppose they would understand it when they heard, while we have been three months at it and don't understand it yet."[1]

We come to the final verses. There has been considerable scholarly attention to this last section of the letter that is our text for the morning. It seems like an abrupt change of tone and topic from the earlier material. One scholar suggests that this does not address the core subject matter of the letter at all, instead—as he put it, it is a "bag of answers to meet recurring problems and questions common to the members of different early Christian communities."[2]

I prefer to think of it as a logical progression from the last two weeks. In the opening chapters, Paul makes the grand theological claims about the centrality of Christ, and then answers the Gnostics and angel worshipers, and the last few weeks have focused on behavior. The claim of Christ should affect our most intimate and private relationships—that was the topic two weeks ago. Last week, we heard Paul declare that the Christian life should impact our relationships at home. Now, the circle widens. This discussion of mutual friends, the "outsiders," the brethren at nearby churches, seems to be a natural next step. How should the Christian life impact relationships beyond the home?

The Gnostics were so consumed with their little clique of "Super Christians" that they did not think much about how to be witnesses to the gospel beyond themselves. Gnosticism narrows their focus to the life and concerns of the "cool kids." It is about our behavior inside the club. Like some stringent Christian traditions today that stay in a frenzy, they protect their little Christian bubble so that no impure influence penetrates. Paul is telling us that the Christian gospel should widen our angle of vision. Through prayer, gracious behavior, and winsome speech, we should think about the gift of good news for others.

Does this strike you as amazing? This says something about Paul. Paul is chained, thrown down into a rock prison, and he writes with the delight of someone filled with warmth and relationship.

Paul writes from a dreary prison cell and yet he is surrounded by a community. He commends them, saying,

- *Tychicus will tell you* about my affairs (v. 7),

- *Onesimus, the faithful and beloved brother* (v. 9),

- *Aristarcus, my fellow prisoner greets you* (v. 10),

- Mark, the cousin of Barnabus, if he comes to you receive him (v. 10).

My tendency is just the opposite. Unlike the imprisoned Paul, I am surrounded by people. I work in a beehive of smart and interesting people. My best friends in the world are close enough for lunch or at least as close as a cell phone call on my way home from work. And yet, I build my own prison. Like the Gnostics, I can become so consumed with my people, my problems, and my little world, that I draw a small circle and cut myself off from life-giving relationships.

Paul talks about how to relate to the "outsider," those who are not Christian. I will go weeks and not see an outsider. I stay on the phone and in meetings with church people. I play with the same toys in the same sandbox with the same friends. And, when I lose my edge, when my world gets small, I stop inviting friends to my sandbox. I stay home. I heat up a Lean Cuisine and look at Facebook to see where my friends are eating dinner and if they liked the grilled snapper, and I tell myself that I am staying connected to the people I care about.

Not to mention that Paul is pushing us out into a world where people are so busy spinning and earning and building and consuming and going and spending and getting in the door and nodding in the elevator and never touching. We each go home to the pain of another day void of meaning or touch—another day filled with people I did not see—another day of crowds, and nobody saw me.

The world is so hungry for the authentic promise of the gospel. The scores of people we pass and nod with are hungry for meaning and belonging and the abundance of the Christian life, and Paul is pushing us to take the Christian life into the world, beyond church and home.

His advice is so simple, and it doesn't require the purchase of DVD's or tracts. The Christian community and booksellers have made this into complicated training, but Paul tells us how to relate to the world beyond our Christian bubble, and it isn't terribly complicated. It is difficult but not complicated. Here's what he says,

> Continue steadfastly in prayer… Walk in wisdom toward outsiders, making the best use of your time. Let your speech always be gracious, seasoned with salt, so that you may know how you ought to answer each person. (vv. 2, 5-6, ESV)

Loosely translated, the first step toward being a gospel witness to the larger community is not to be a jerk. How about making friends?

- "Pray."

- "Make the most of your time" with other people; be fully present.

- "Be gracious"; be the person others hope they get to sit with at lunch.

- "Know how you ought to answer." That is, when the matter of faith, meaning, church, purpose, fullness, or delight comes naturally into conversation, know how to answer with a gracious word that bears witness to the truth.

As Anne Lamott says, "…you don't always have to chop with the sword of truth. You can point with it, too."[3]

Paul's advice in dealing with the non-Christian world is to "Be gracious".

I heard Dr. Fred Craddock, now retired Professor of Preaching at Emory, say, "The final work of grace in a person's life is to make him or her gracious." Perhaps that's true.

Would people describe you as gracious? Have you given any thought to whether or not you are the one people want to sit with at lunch? I have a pastor friend who actually divides people into two groups. One is the group of people who give her energy when she is around them. The other group is the people who completely drain her. When she schedules meetings for her week, she will never schedule more than three meetings in a week with people who drain her energy. It is one way she takes care of herself. She tries to fill her week with people who fill her and energize her and minimize her time with the drains on her emotional energy. (I'd tell you how this is working for her, but I can't seem to get on her lunch schedule.)

> *Walk in wisdom toward outsiders, making the best use of the time. Let your speech always be gracious, seasoned with salt, so that you may know how you ought to answer each person.* (vv. 5-6, ESV)

An early writing, the Apocalypse of Sedrach, says that no respectable person, when hosting others, would serve a meal without salt. Apparently, in the ancient world, there was an association with "salt" and "enjoyment."[4] *Let your speech always be gracious, seasoned with salt* (v. 6).

This sermon might be beginning to sound like a Hallmark card. It isn't one. Let me assure you that this is muscular work, which is why Paul begins with prayer. If you turn loose wisdom and gracious speech—if you begin to widen the circle and look for ways to include people in your graciousness, it will start to look radical, not pastel and nice. Being gracious has the power to reform relationships.

Consider a few of the names Paul mentions:

- Onesimus, whom we know from another letter, was a slave. And yet, Paul does not call him a slave here at all. He is called faithful and beloved brother. Transformed relationship. (v. 9)

- Mark, the cousin of Barnabas, do you remember him? The Book of Acts records Mark and the Apostle Paul's relational spat. He quit on Paul once, and Paul refused to take him on another journey. They never worked together again. And yet, here, he says to the Colossians, *if he comes to you, welcome him* (v. 10). Transformed relationship.

- Or, as Paul mentioned in verse 11, only a few of his fellow workers were men *of the circumcision.* Gentiles who were once racial "outsiders" Paul has now included in his circle of care. Transformed relationship.

- Or Nympha, who is the leader of a church in her home. A first-century, marginalized woman is extended greetings from the apostle. Transformed relationship. (v. 15)

Who is the hardest person for you to be gracious toward? It is probably someone on this list.

- Slaves now free, that is, someone not in your social standing?

- Mark, someone you once had a falling out with?

- The uncircumcised, somebody of a different ethnic background?

- Or Nympha, someone that the Christian community has generally looked down on?

Being gracious is not the soft work of a Hallmark card. It is the hard, gritty, generous, loving response to having been set free.

> Continue steadfastly in prayer… Walk in wisdom toward outsiders, making the best use of your time. Let your speech always be gracious, seasoned with salt, so that you may know how you ought to answer each person. (vv. 2, 5-6, ESV)

You have been set free. By the power of the gospel, you have experienced forgiveness and purpose and genuine community. Some of you have been in church so long that you don't remember a time that you were an "outsider." But some of you do. You remember driving by churches and wondering what kind of hocus-pocus happens in there. You remember wondering if you would be welcome, included. You remember feeling some tug that the answer to life might be found in the message proclaimed behind the stained glass, but you were not sure if you would find a welcome place. You might remember wishing someone would invite you. You might have been scared that someone would invite you. Each story is different. The stories about how you found your way from outside to inside are varied. But I'll bet there is one common experience—one thing that got you here and kept you coming—you met someone who was gracious.

NOTES

1. "Concerning the Ministry" (London: Student Christian Movement Press, 1936), 236, quoted in Frances W. Beare, "The Epistle to the Colossians: Exegesis," *The Interpreter's Bible*, Vol. 11 (Nashville: Abingdon Press, 1955), 234.

2. D. G. Bradley, "The Topos as a Form in the Pauline Paraenesis," *JBL* 72 (1953): 246, quoted in Nijay K. Gupta, *Colossians*, Smyth & Helwys Commentary (Macon, GA: Smyth & Helwys Publishing, 2013), 183.

3. Anne Lamott, *Bird by Bird: Some Instructions on Writing and Life* (New York: Anchor Books, 1995), 156.

4. Nijay K. Gupta, *Colossians*, Smyth & Helwys Commentary (Macon, GA: Smyth & Helwys Publishing, 2013), 190.

www.ingramcontent.com/pod-product-compliance
Lightning Source LLC
Chambersburg PA
CBHW062215080426
42734CB00010B/1901